Herzlich willkommen bei Familie Lerndrache!

Super, dass du mit uns üben und lernen möchtest! Du wirst sehen: Mit uns macht das richtig viel Spaß! Wir haben viele Tipps für dich und helfen dir, sodass du bald fit in Englisch bist.

Name: Lizzy Lerndrache
Das mag ich: Sport, vor allem Reiten und Ballett; schöne Kleider und meine Perlenkette; meine Familie, besonders meinen Bruder Lenny (meistens jedenfalls)
So bin ich: erfinderisch und ganz schön schlau

Name: Lenny Lerndrache
Das mag ich: Sport; alles, was mit Technik zu tun hat; Feuer spucken; meine Familie, besonders meine Schwester Lizzy (meistens jedenfalls)
So bin ich: hilfsbereit und neugierig

Name: Floh Lerndrache (Baby)
Das mag ich: Quatsch!
So bin ich: frech und noch klein, daher kann ich kaum reden und leider noch nicht fliegen

Name: Nepomuk Lerndrache (Opa)
Das mag ich: fliegen und Saltos schlagen; mit meinem Stock zaubern; faulenzen; meine Enkelkinder
So bin ich: gemütlich, manchmal kann ich auch richtig frech sein

Inhalt

Das bedeuten die unterschiedlichen Zeichen:

Spure die hell gedruckten Buchstaben nach.
Fülle die Lücken im Text!

Kreuze an!

Hier kannst du ausmalen!

Lies laut, was hier steht!

Dieses Lied kannst du dir auf der CD anhören!

Hello !

1

What's your name?

1

How are you?

1

Hello, Oliver, how are you?
I'm fine, thanks.
Hello, I'm Lilian. I'm not very well.
Poor Lilian, goodbye.
G________,
p____
L_______.

What is he doing?

1

What's Oliver doing?

He's skate-boarding. I'm skateboarding, too.

What's Paul doing?

He's dancing.

Yes, I'm __________.

I'm not sk ____________.

I'm not d ________.

I am reading.

What are they doing?

1 

	yes	no
Is Peter skateboarding?	☐	☐
Is Julia dancing?	☐	☐
Is Dolly reading?	☐	☐

2 

Look, there's Dolly.

She's d_ _ _ _ _ _ _ _ _ _.

Look, th_ _ _ _ '_ _ _ _ _ _ _ _ _ _.

He's _.

Who's this?

hello name reading reading is Nicky

My paintbox

1

2

3

4

Chocolate is b_ _ _ _.

An orange is _ _ _ _ _ _.

The sun is _ _ _ _ _ _.

A tomato is _ _ _.

Grass is _ _ _ _ _.

Snow is _ _ _ _ _.

From one to ten

1 

one two three four five

six seven eight nine ten

2 

3

I've got three friends.
How many friends
have you got?

I've got ____________ ______________.

4

My friends

name

____________	____________
____________	____________
____________	____________
____________	____________
____________	____________
____________	____________
____________	____________
____________	____________
____________	____________
____________	____________
____________	____________

My birthday party

It is Donald's birthday. Donald is 11 years old.

1

It's not my birthday.
It's Donald's birthday.

I am Donald.
It's my ____________ .

It's his
____________ .

Kay is 8 years old.
Susan is 7 years old.
I am 10. And you?
How old are you?

2

I am

________ ________ _______.

3

4

More colours

1  

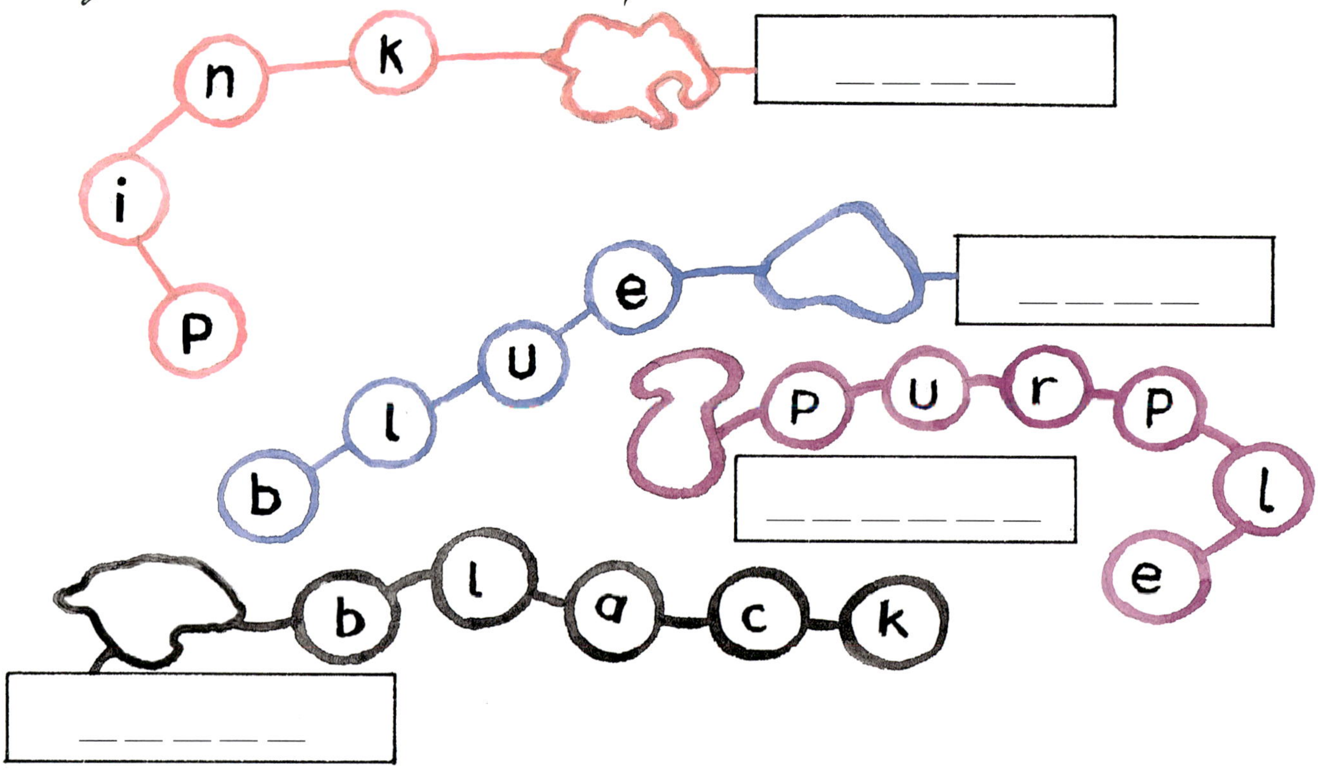

2 

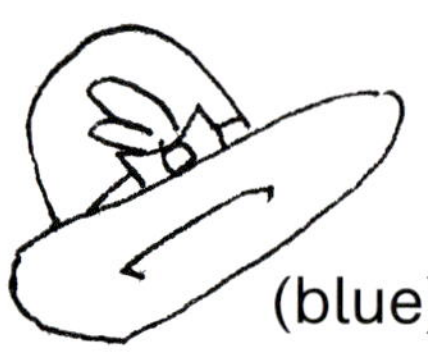
(blue)

(black)

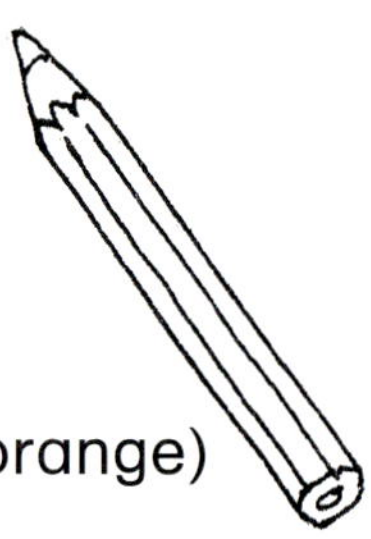
(orange)

(purple)
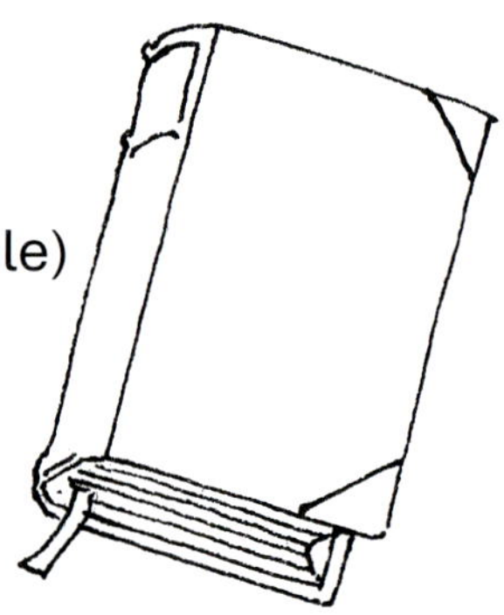

(yellow)

(red)

3

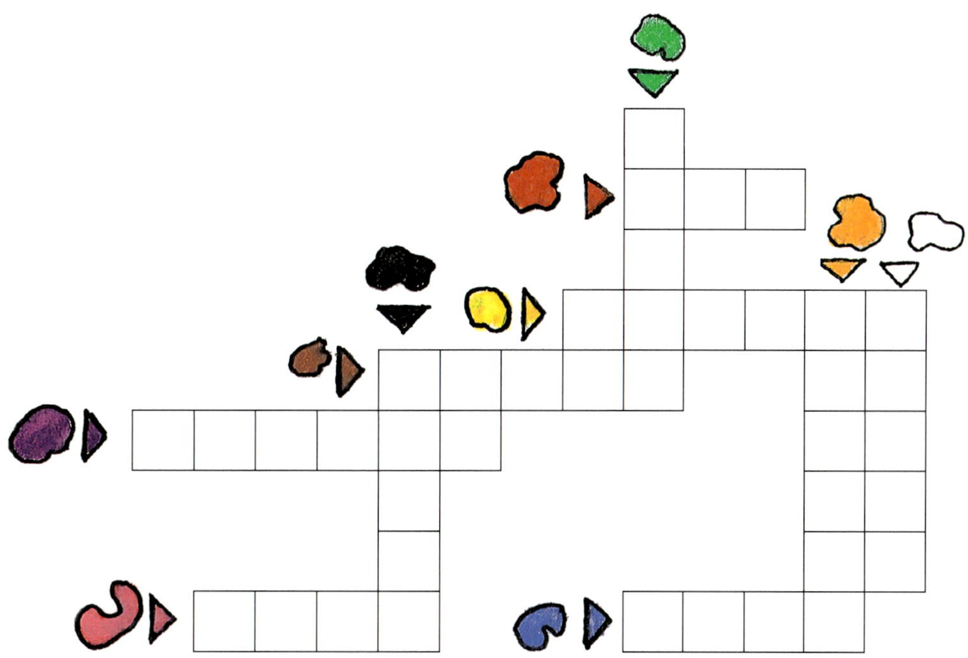

4

Toby's pullover is __________ .

Toby's cab is __________ .

Toby's short's are __________ .

Toby's shoes are __________ .

Animals, animals, animals

1

1/h 3/e 2/p 5/s 4/u 7/a 6/f 9/c 8/y 12/o 11/t 10/n 13/r 14/d 16/i 15/g 17/m 18/k

a) □□□
14 12 15

b) □□□
9 7 11

d) □□□□
2 12 10 8

c) □□□
2 16 15

e) □□□□□□□
1 7 17 5 11 3 13

f) □□□□
14 4 9 18

g) □□□□
6 16 5 1

2 Do you have a pet?

I have a hamster.
I like my hamster.

I have a ______.
I like m__ c___.

I h____ __ f______.
I______ ____ ______.

I______ __ ______.
__ ______ _____ ______.

3 What pet do you have?

I have a ____________________.

At school

1 One, two, three …

2 Where are they?

The computer is on the table.

Lizzy is beside the table.

The cat is under the table.

3

Where is the chair?

The chair is ________ the table.

Where is Tommy?

________ _____ _____ the chair.

Where is David?

________ _____ _____ ______ ________.

Where is the little Floh?

He is ________ ______ ________.

And where are you?

I am ______________________________.

Our clothes

1  What is it?

2 Have you got a ...?

3 yellow, blue, red, green
Pullover, socks, hat, shorts

My body

1  This is Tom.

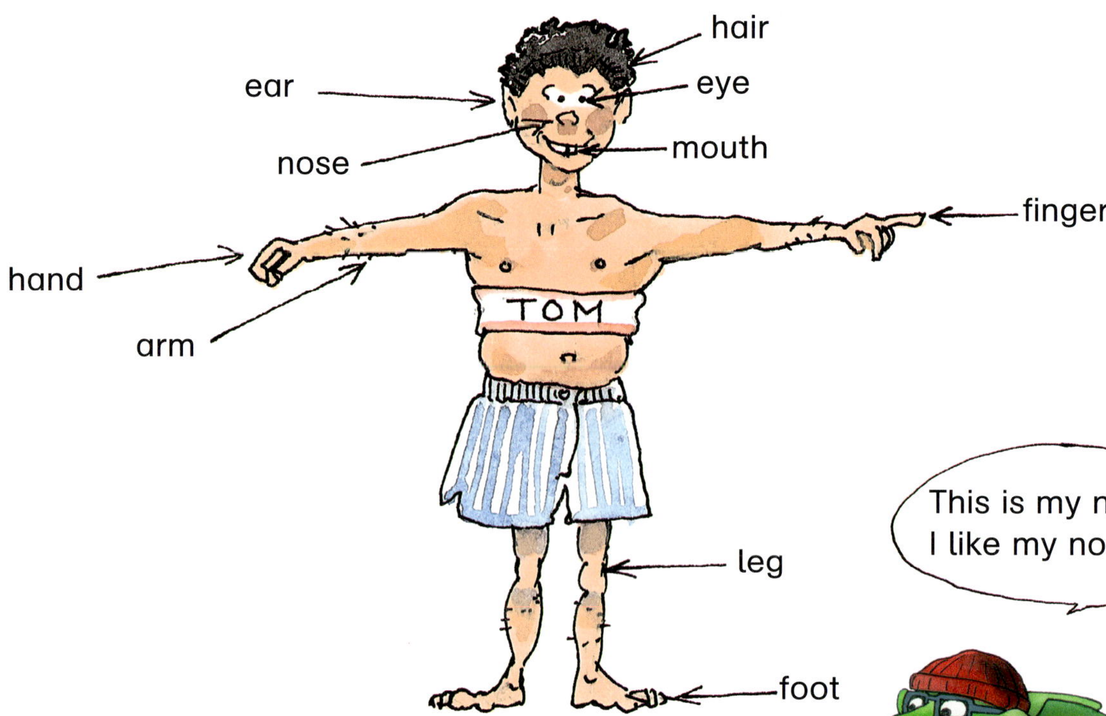

2 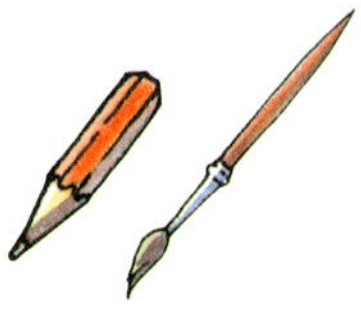 This is Tom's friend Susan.

3

two eyes one eye

two ears one ______

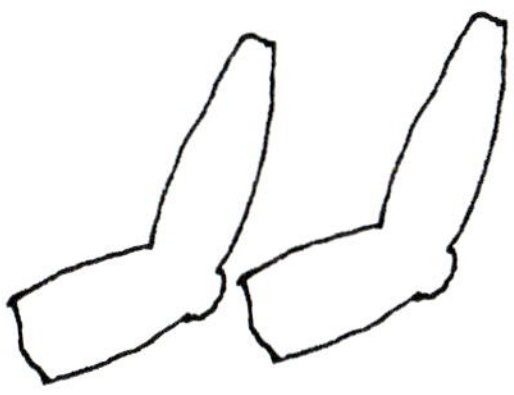

two arms one ______

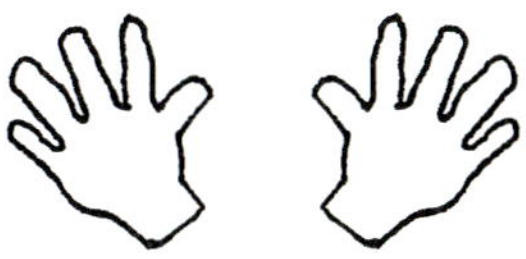

two hands o___ ______

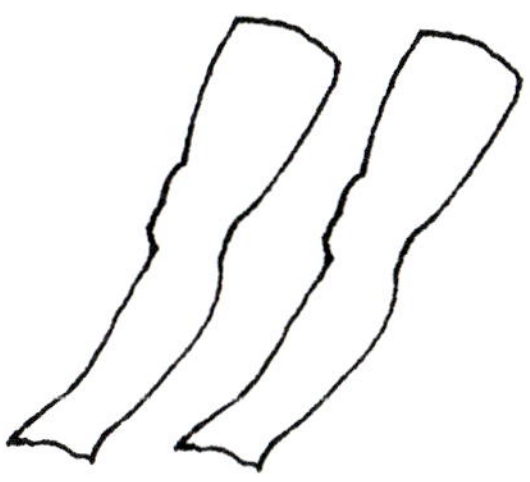

two legs ______ ______

two feet ______ ______

4

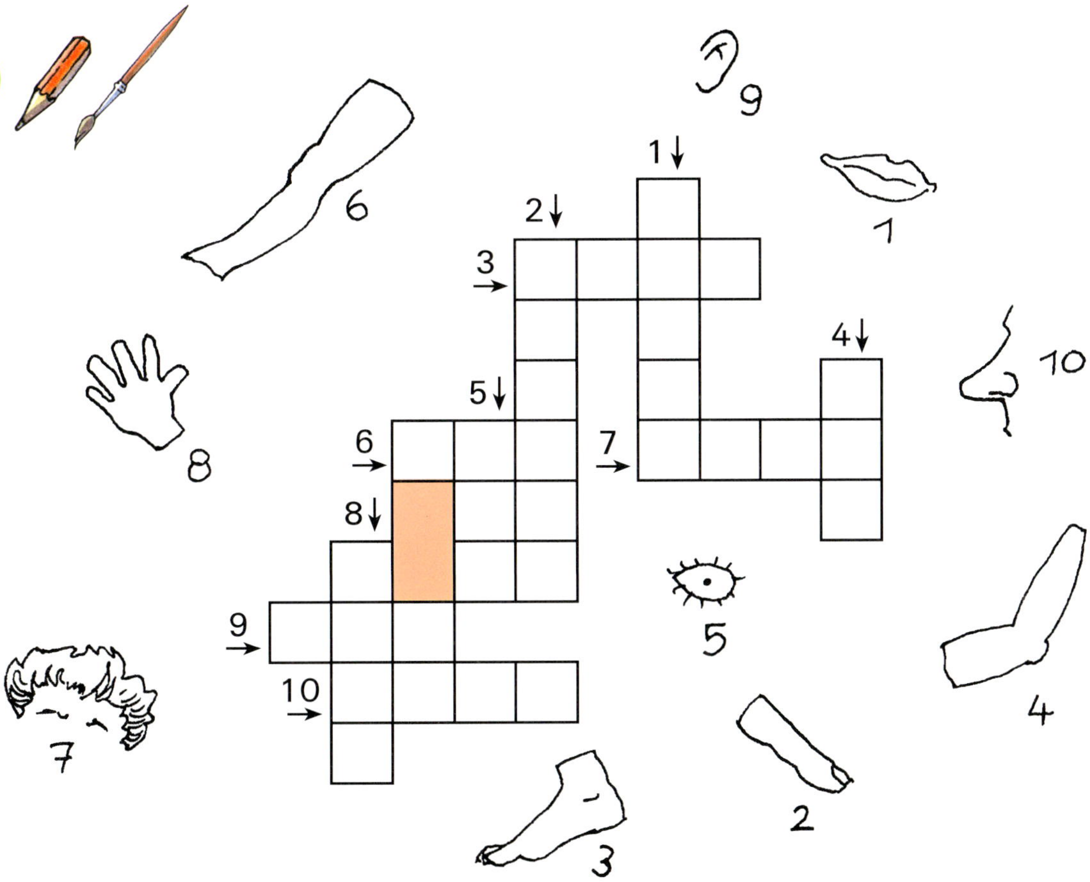

My family

1

2

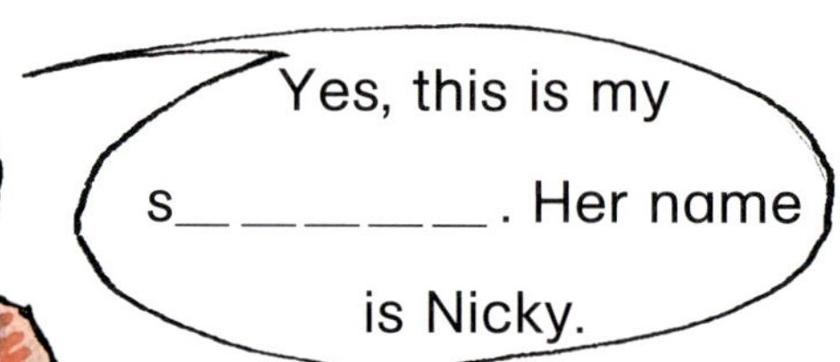

Nicky's hair is ________ .

Her brother's hair is ________ .

3

sisters brothers years

Do you have a brother?

Yes I do. He is ten ________ old.

Do you have a sister?

No, I don't.
I haven't any ________
or ________ .

4

My sister has a dog.

My brother has
___ ____________ .

My grandpa has
___ ____________ .

In my room

1

2

This is my bed.

This is my ____________________.

This i__ ____ ____________________.

______________________________.

______________________________.

______________________________.

3

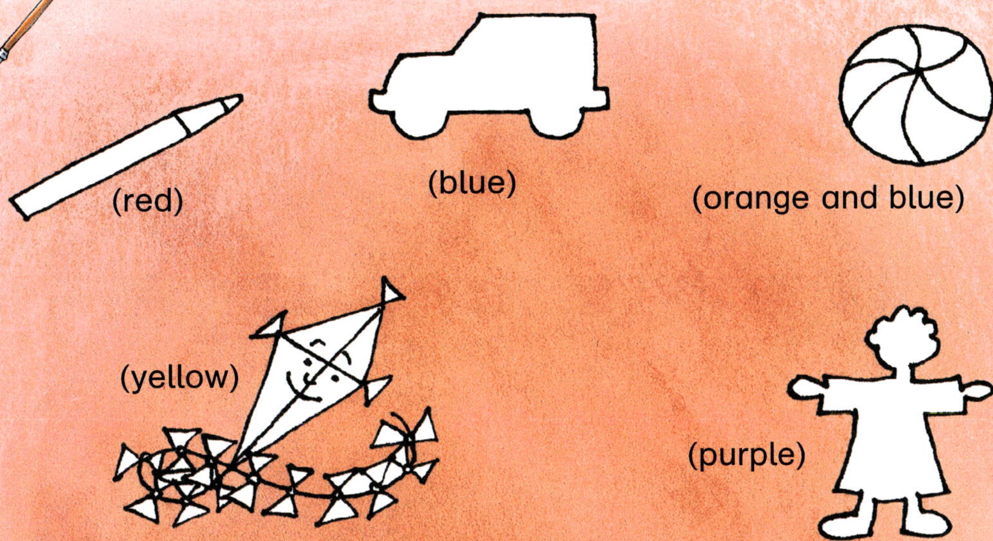

4

5 (blue ball)

A day with Tom and Dolly

1

They get up at seven o'clock.

They go to school at ________ o'clock.

They play at ________ o'clock.

They have dinner at ________ o'clock.

They watch TV at half past six.

They go to bed at ________ ________ ________.
Good night!

2 Now it is your turn. Tell about your day.

I am ______________ .

I get up ______________________________ .

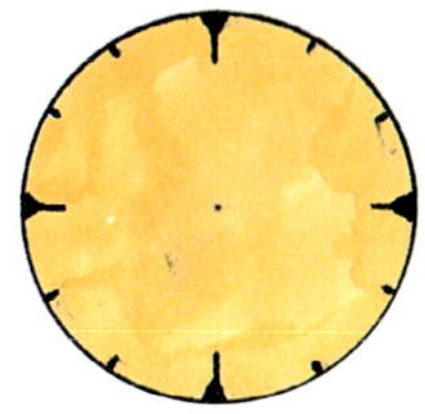

I go ______________________________

______________________________ .

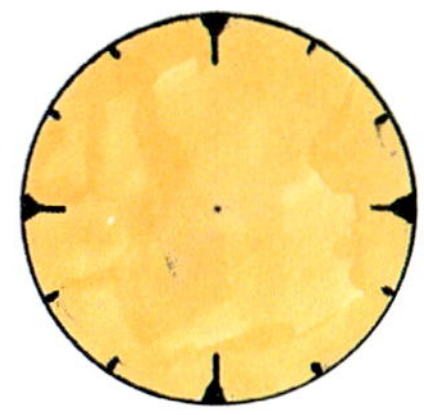

I ______________________________

______________________________ .

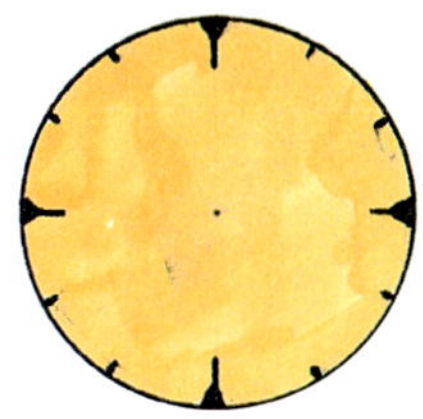

____

______________________________ .

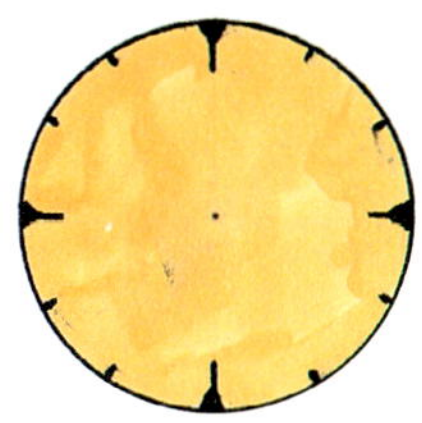

____

______________________________ .

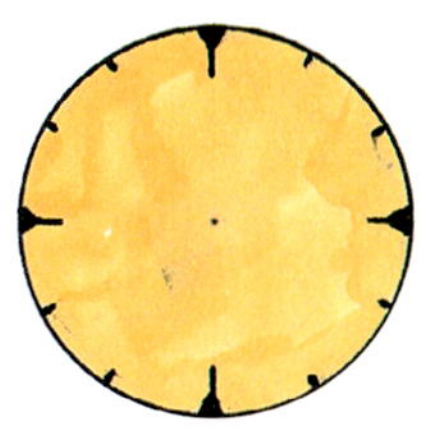

____

______________________________ .

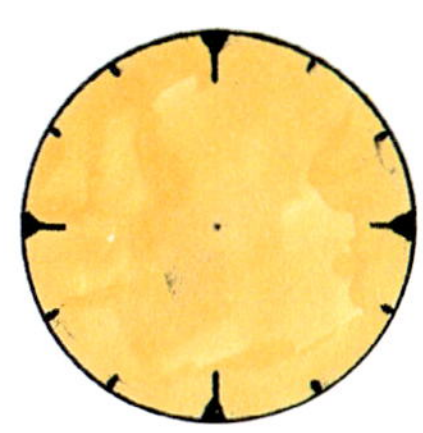

One elephant went out to play

One elephant went out to play,
Out on a spider's web one day.
He had such enormous fun,
He called for another elephant to come.

Two elephants went out to play,
Out on a spider's web one day.
They had such enormous fun,
They called for another elephant to come.

Three elephants went out to play,
Out on a spider's web one day.
They had such enormous fun,
They called for another elephant to come.

Four elephants went out to play,
Out on a spider's web one day.
They had such enormous fun,
They called for another elephant to come.

Five elephants went out to play,
Out on a spider's web one day.
They had such enormous fun,
Playing all together in the sun.

went out to play	ging spielen
spider	Spinne
web	Netz
day	Tag
enormous	enorm, riesig
fun	Spaß
called for	forderte auf
another	ein anderer
come	kommen
play, playing	spielen
all together	alle zusammen
sun	Sonne

1

Six elephants went out to ____________ ,
Out on a ____________'s web one _________ .
_________ had such ______________ fun,
They called for ______________ elephant to ______________ .

2

__ __ __ __ __ __ __ __   __ __ __
2 4 2 7 6 8 3 1   5 13 14

__ __ __ __ __ __ __ __ __
9 7 11 5 2 10 12 8 1

8 = a
6 = h
2 = e
7 = p
9 = s
13 = o
12 = c
3 = n
5 = d
10 = r
11 = i
1 = t
4 = l
14 = g

3

dog|catelephantcatmousedogcatdogspiderelephant

	Yes	No
There are three dogs.		
There is one cat.		
There are four elephants.		
There is one mouse.		
There is one spider.		

Eency weency spider

The eency weency spider
Went up the water spout.

Down came the rain
And washed the spider out.

Out came the sun
And dried up all the rain.

And the eency weency spider
Went up the spout again.

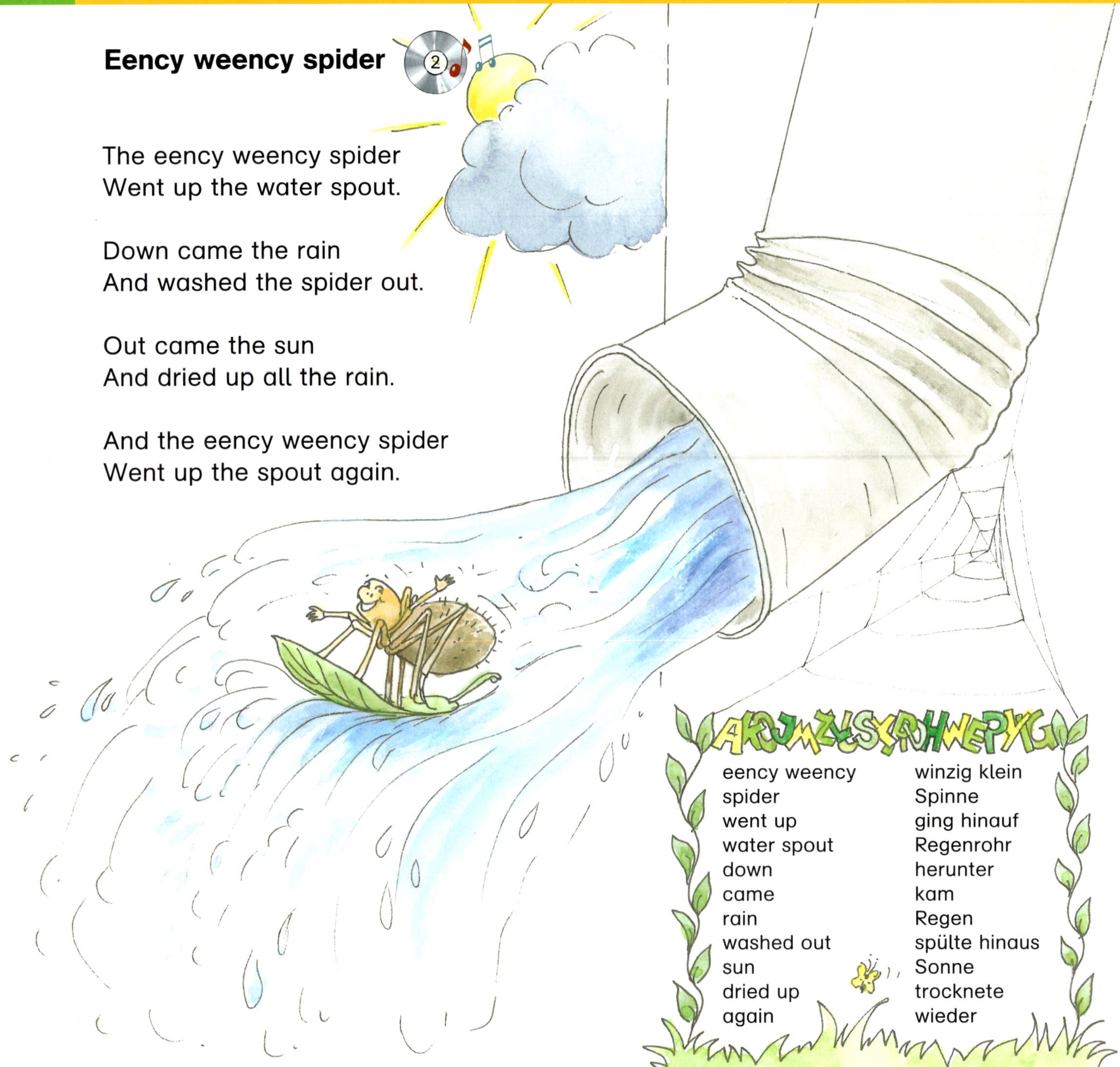

eency weency	winzig klein
spider	Spinne
went up	ging hinauf
water spout	Regenrohr
down	herunter
came	kam
rain	Regen
washed out	spülte hinaus
sun	Sonne
dried up	trocknete
again	wieder

1

A	Z	R	A	I	N
W	O	P	F	S	K
I	S	U	N	H	A
N	R	S	N	O	W
D	E	X	I	S	Q
I	C	L	O	U	D

 ________________

 ________________

 ________________

 ________________

 ________________

2

spring

____

____

____

3

Christmas is in	summer/autumn/winter/spring.
Easter is in	winter/spring/summer/autumn.
Halloween is in	spring/summer/autumn/winter.
Summer holidays are in	autumn/spring/summer/winter.

This old man

This old man, he played **one**,
He played knick-knack **on my thumb**.
With a knick-knack paddywhack,
Give the dog a bone.
This old man came rolling home.

Two – on my shoe
Three – on my knee
Four – on my door
Five – on my hive
Six – on my sticks
Seven – up to heaven
Eight – on my gate
Nine – on my spine
Ten – once again

this	dieser	rolling home	nach Hause rollen
old man	alter Mann	shoe	Schuh
play	spielen	knee	Knie
knick-knack	Spielerei	door	Tür
thumb	Daumen	hive	Bienenkorb
paddywhack	Krimskrams	sticks	Stöcke
give	geben	heaven	Himmel
dog	Hund	gate	Tor
bone	Knochen	spine	Rückgrat
came	kam	once again	nochmals

1

2

Sara says, "Tom is my ______________.
Ann is my ______________.
Mike is my ______________.
Susan is my ______________.
Robin is my ______________.
Kevin is my ______________.
I'm Robin and Kevin's ______________."

3

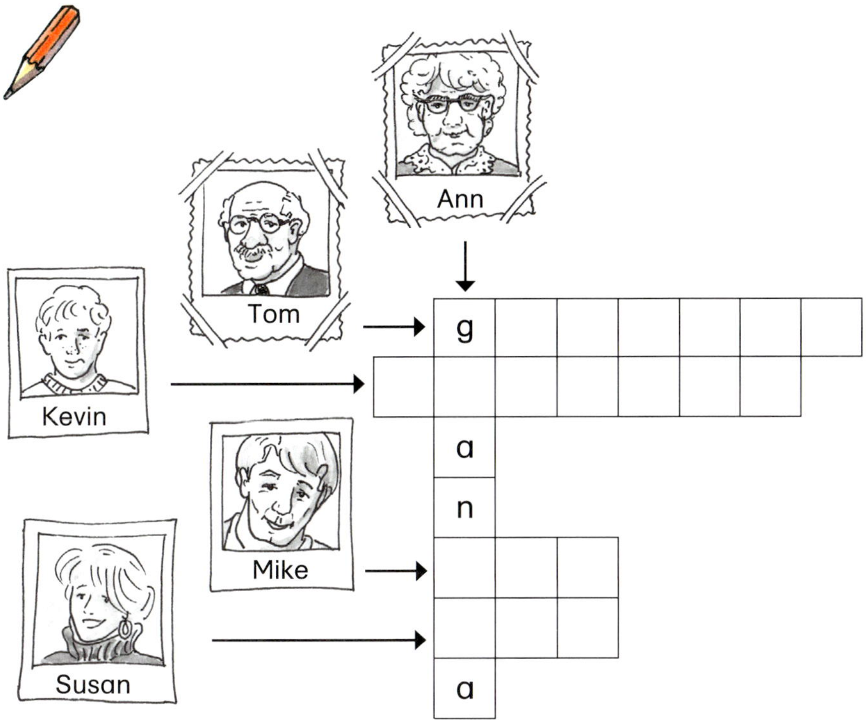

4

Sara is missing. She is Robin and Kevin's ____________.

Old Mac Donald had a farm 

Old MacDonald had a farm, E-I-E-I-O!
And on his farm he had some **chicks**, E-I-E-I-O!
With a **chick, chick** here, and a **chick, chick** there,
Here a **chick**, there a **chick**, everywhere a **chick, chick**.
Old MacDonald had a farm, E-I-E-I-O!

Old MacDonald had a farm, E-I-E-I-O!
And on his farm he had some **cows**, E-I-E-I-O!
With a **moo, moo** here, and a **moo, moo** there,
Here a **moo**, there a **moo**, everywhere a **moo, moo**.
Old MacDonald had a farm, E-I-E-I-O!

Old MacDonald had a farm, E-I-E-I-O!
And on his farm he had some **pigs**, E-I-E-I-O!
With an **oink, oink** here, and an **oink, oink** there,
Here an **oink**, there an **oink**, everywhere an **oink, oink**.
Old MacDonald had a farm, E-I-E-I-O!

Sheep – baa, baa
Ducks – quack, quack

old	alt
farm	Bauernhof
some	ein paar
chicks	Küken
with	mit
here	hier
there	da, dort
everywhere	überall
cows	Kühe
pigs	Schweine
sheep	Schafe
ducks	Enten

1 

farm – cow – grass – ~~banana~~ – farmhouse – farmer

dog – sheep – duck – pig – train – horse

quack – woof – miaow – moo – oink – hello

2

3

	Yes	No
moo – sheep		
oink – cow		
baa – duck		
quack – pig		
woof – dog		

4

one cow – two ____________________

one hamster – four ____________________

one spider – three ____________________

one cat – five ____________________

one rabbit – seven ____________________

Hickory, dickory, dock

Hickory, dickory, dock,
The **mouse** went up the clock.
The clock struck **one**,
Down he did run.
Hickory, dickory, dock.

Fly – two – away he flew
Frog – three – the frog did flee
Worm – four – he fell to the floor
Bee – five – he flew to the hive
Snake – six – he hid in some sticks
Moth – seven – he flew to the heavens
Cricket – eight – he hid in a crate
Spider – nine – he swung down his line
Mole – ten – he ran to his den
Ant – eleven – he hid behind seven
Elephant – twelve – he let out a yell
Last line – and that was the end of the clock.

mouse	Maus	moth	Motte
went up	ging hinauf	heaven	Himmel
clock	Uhr	cricket	Grille
struck	schlug	crate	Lattenkiste
down	hinunter	spider	Spinne
did run	rannte	swung	baumelte
fly	Fliege	line	Faden
flew away	flog weg	mole	Maulwurf
frog	Frosch	ran	rannte
did flee	floh	den	Höhle
worm	Wurm	ant	Ameise
fell	fiel	behind	hinter
floor	Boden	elephant	Elefant
bee	Biene	let out	stieß aus
hive	Bienenkorb	yell	Schrei
snake	Schlange	last line	letzte Zeile
hid	versteckte sich	end	Ende
sticks	Stöcke		

1

breakfast lunch tea dinner

B ________________ is at ____________ o'clock.

L ________________ is at ____________ o'clock.

T ________________ is at ____________ o'clock.

D ________________ is at ____________ o'clock.

2

Lenny Lizzy Baby Floh

Lenny plays basketball at ________ o'clock.

Lizzy has lunch at ________ o'clock.

Baby Floh goes to bed at ________ o'clock.

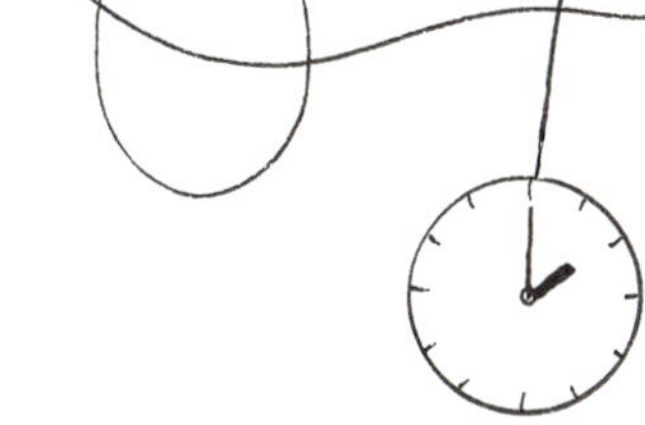

Little Boy Blue

Little Boy Blue,
Come blow your horn,
The sheep's in the meadow;
The cow's in the corn.

But where is the boy
Who looks after the sheep?
He's under the haystack,
Fast asleep.

Will you wake him?
No, not I.
For if I do,
He's sure to cry.

little	klein	but	aber
boy	Junge	where	wo
blue	blau	look after	aufpassen
come	kommen	under	unter
blow	blasen	haystack	Heuhaufen
horn	Horn	fast	schnell
sheep	Schaf(e)	asleep	eingeschlafen
meadow	Wiese	wake	wecken
cow	Kuh	sure	sicher
corn	Maisfeld	cry	weinen

1

2

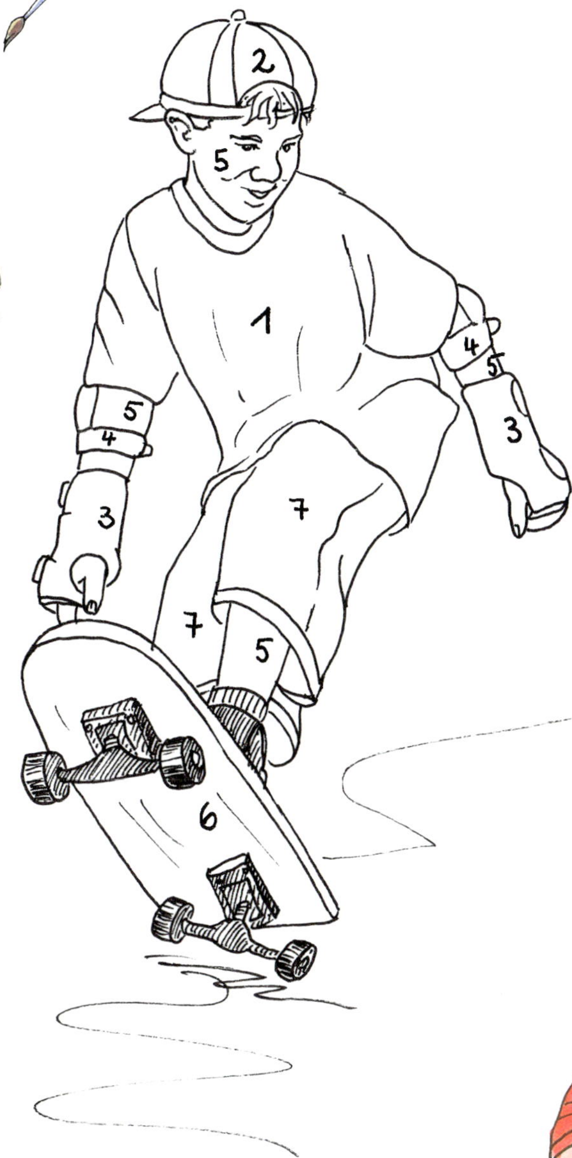

1 = green
2 = red
3 = blue
4 = yellow
5 = pink
6 = purple
7 = brown

3

Her eyes are blue.
Her hair is black.
Her T-shirt is red.
Her jeans are blue.
Her shoes are green.

Her name is ______________ .

A-hunting we will go 

Oh, a-hunting we will go,
A-hunting we will go,
We'll catch a fox
And put him in a box,
and then we'll let him go!

Oh, a-hunting we will go,
A-hunting we will go,
We'll catch a cat
And put him in a hat,
And then we'll let him go!

Oh, a-hunting we will go,
A-hunting we will go,
We'll catch a mouse
And put him in a house,
And then we'll let him go!

Oh, a-hunting we will go,
A-hunting we will go,
We'll catch a goat
And put him in a boat,
And then we'll let him go!

hunting	jagen
we will go	wir werden gehen
catch	fangen
fox	Fuchs
box	Schachtel
let	lassen
cat	Katze
hat	Hut
mouse	Maus
house	Haus
goat	Ziege
boat	Boot

1

The fox is in the ________ .

The mouse is in the ____________ .

The ________ is in the boat.

The ________ is in the hat.

2

I like  I don't like 

 singing songs ◯

watching TV ◯ 

 learning English ◯

swimming ◯ 

 reading a book ◯

riding my bike ◯ 

3

☐ Ron is fishing.

☐ Susan is sailing.

☐ Mike is surfing.

☐ Mandy is playing tennis.

☐ Carol is singing.

☐ Tom is swimming.

1

2

3

4

5

6

Mary had a little lamb

Mary had a little lamb, little lamb, little lamb,
Mary had a little lamb. Its fleece was white as snow.

And everywhere that Mary went, Mary went, Mary went,
Everywhere that Mary went the lamb was sure to go.

It followed her to school one day, school one day, school one day.
It followed her to school one day. That was against the rule.

It made the children laugh and play, laugh and play, laugh and play.
It made the children laugh and play to see a lamb at school.

The teacher said what shall we do, shall we do, shall we do?
The teacher said what shall we do? This lamb has come to school.

Let's teach her how to read and write, read and write, read and write.
Let's teach her how to read and write and learn the golden rule.

Mary's lamb now teaches school, teaches school, teaches school.
Mary's lamb now teaches school on her grandpa's farm.

little	klein	play	spielen
lamb	Lamm	see	sehen
fleece	Fell	teacher	Lehrer
white	weiß	said	sagte
snow	Schnee	what	was
everywhere	überall	come	kommen
went	ging	teach	unterrichten
sure	sicher	read	lesen
go	gehen	write	schreiben
followed	folgte	golden	golden
school	Schule	grandpa	Großvater
against the rule	gegen die Regel	farm	Bauernhof
laugh	lachen		

1

a board
a book
a pencil

a box
a pencil case
a pencil

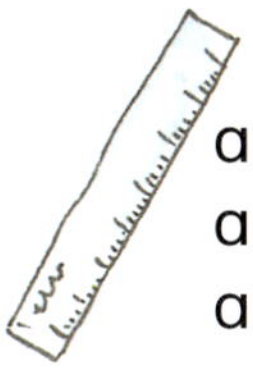

a ruler
a rubber
a sharpener

a basket
a schoolbag
a plastic bag

a book
a pen
a felt tip

2

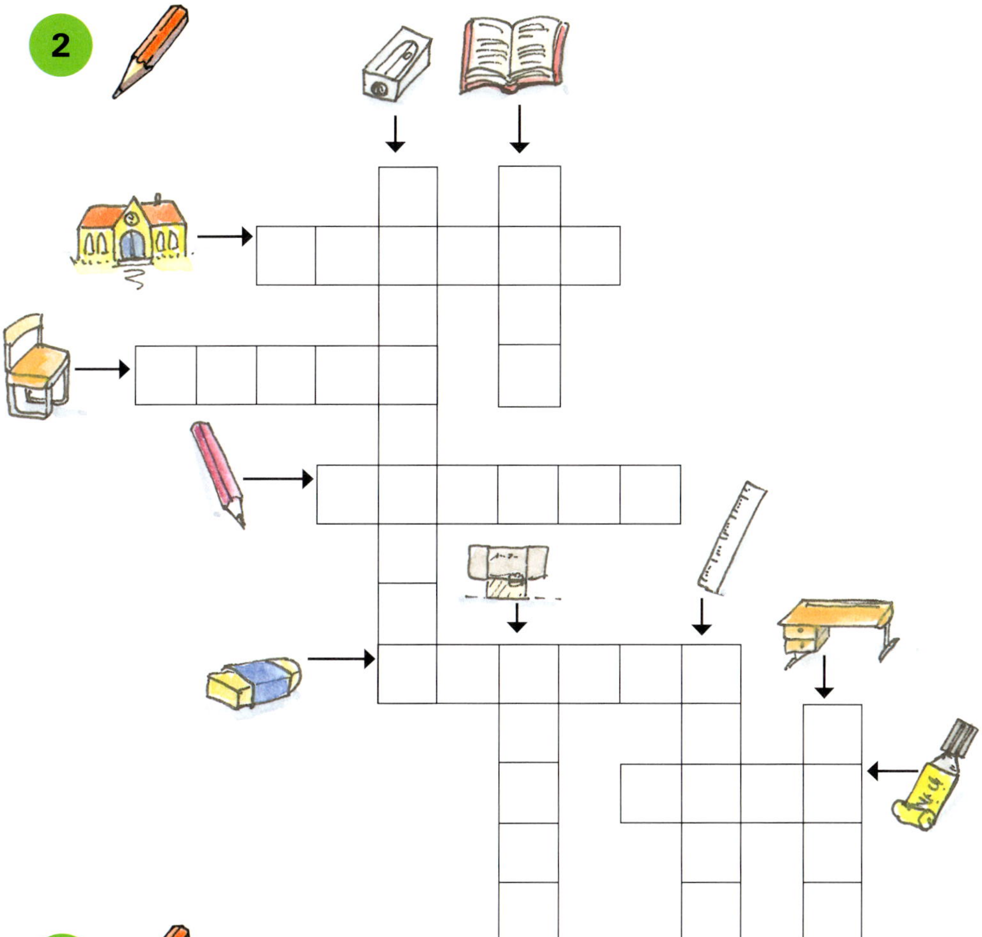

→ school
glue
pencil
rubber
chair

↓ desk
ruler
sharpener
board
book

3

There are ☐ rulers. 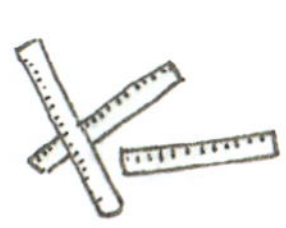

There are ☐ pencils. 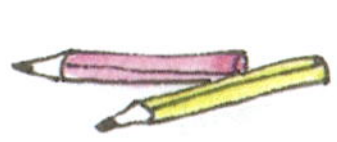

There are ☐ books. 

There are ☐ scissors. 

There is ☐ schoolbag. 

There is ☐ sharpener. 

There is ☐ pencil case. 

There is ☐ glue. 

Teddy bear

Teddy bear, teddy bear, turn around.
Teddy bear, teddy bear, touch the ground.

Teddy bear, teddy bear, show your shoe.
Teddy bear, teddy bear, that will do.

Teddy bear, teddy bear, go to bed.
Teddy bear, teddy bear, rest your head.

Teddy bear, teddy bear, turn out the light.
Teddy bear, teddy bear, say good night.

teddy bear	Teddybär	go to bed	zu Bett gehen
turn around	sich drehen	rest	ausruhen
touch	berühren	head	Kopf
ground	Boden	turn out	ausschalten
show	zeigen	light	Licht
shoe	Schuh	say	sagen
do	tun	good night	gute Nacht

1

2

2/o 1/i 4/h 13/a 8/d 7/b 14/k 3/t 15/u 5/s 6/g 11/r 12/m 18/n 19/l 9/c 16/p 17/y 10/e

4 ___ 2 ___ 11 ___ 5 ___ 10 ___

13 ___ 18 ___ 3 ___

12 ___ 2 ___ 15 ___ 5 ___ 10 ___

5 ___ 18 ___ 13 ___ 14 ___ 10 ___

3 ___ 10 ___ 8 ___ 8 ___ 17 ___ 7 ___ 10 ___ 13 ___ 11 ___

10 ___ 19 ___ 10 ___ 16 ___ 4 ___ 13 ___ 18 ___ 3 ___

11 ___ 13 ___ 7 ___ 7 ___ 1 ___ 3 ___

= 4 ___ 13 ___ 12 ___ 5 ___ 3 ___ 10 ___ 11 ___

3

How many animals are there in this bed?

There are ☐ monkeys in this bed.

There are ☐ dogs in this bed.

There are ☐ ducks in this bed.

There is ☐ snake in this bed.

One, two, buckle my shoe

One, two,
Buckle my shoe;

Three, four,
Shut the door;

Five, six,
Pick up sticks;

Seven, eight,
Lay them straight;

Nine, ten,
A big fat hen.

one, two	eins, zwei	sticks	Holzstöcke
buckle	schnüren	seven, eight	sieben, acht
shoe	Schuh	lay	legen
three, four	drei, vier	straight	gerade
shut	schließen	nine, ten	neun, zehn
door	Tür	big	groß
five, six	fünf, sechs	fat	fett
pick up	auflesen	hen	Henne

1

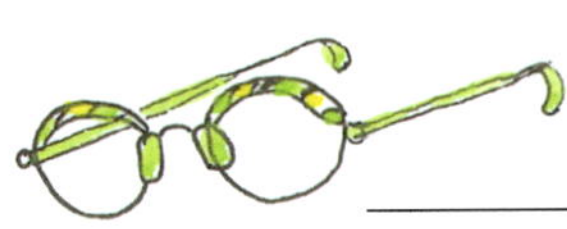

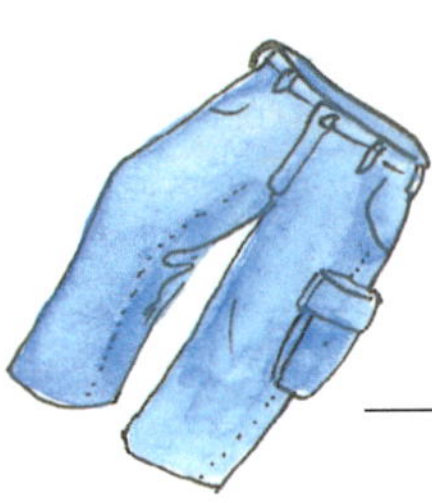

2

3

One spider has got ☐ legs.

Two cows have got ☐ legs.

Three birds have got ☐ legs.

Four horses have got ☐ legs.

Five rabbits have got ☐ legs.

One duck has got ☐ legs.

The cat came piping out of the barn

The cat came piping out of the barn,
With a set of bagpipes under her arm.
She could sing nothing but "Fiddle-de-dee",
The mouse will marry the bumblebee.
Cat plays bagpipes.
Bee dances with mouse.
We'll have the wedding at our good house.

The cat came piping out of the barn.
As the cow and the sow danced arm in arm.
The ducks in their waistcoats served biscuits and tea,
For the mouse had married the bumblebee.
They'll live in a hole
In the old chestnut tree,
Fiddle-de-dee, fiddle-de-dee.

cat	Katze	bumblebee	Hummel	waistcoat	Weste
came	kam	play	spielen	served	servierte
piping	pfeifend	bee	Biene	biscuits	Kekse
barn	Scheune	dance	tanzen	tea	Tee
bagpipes	Dudelsack	have	haben	live	leben
could	konnte	wedding	Hochzeit	hole	Höhle
nothing but	nur	cow	Kuh	old	alt
mouse	Maus	sow	Sau	chestnut tree	Kastanienbaum
marry	heiraten	duck	Ente		

1

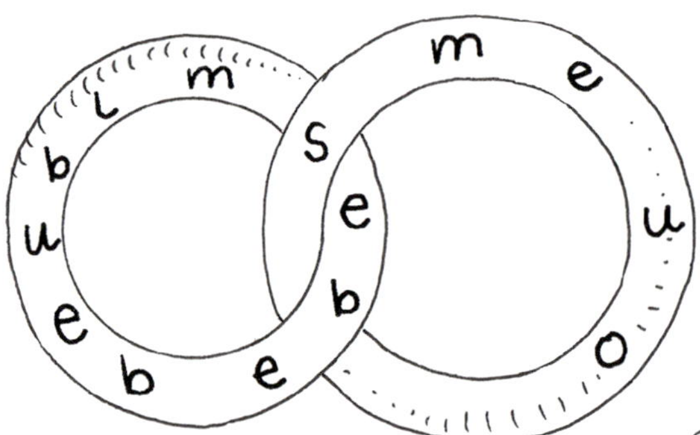

2

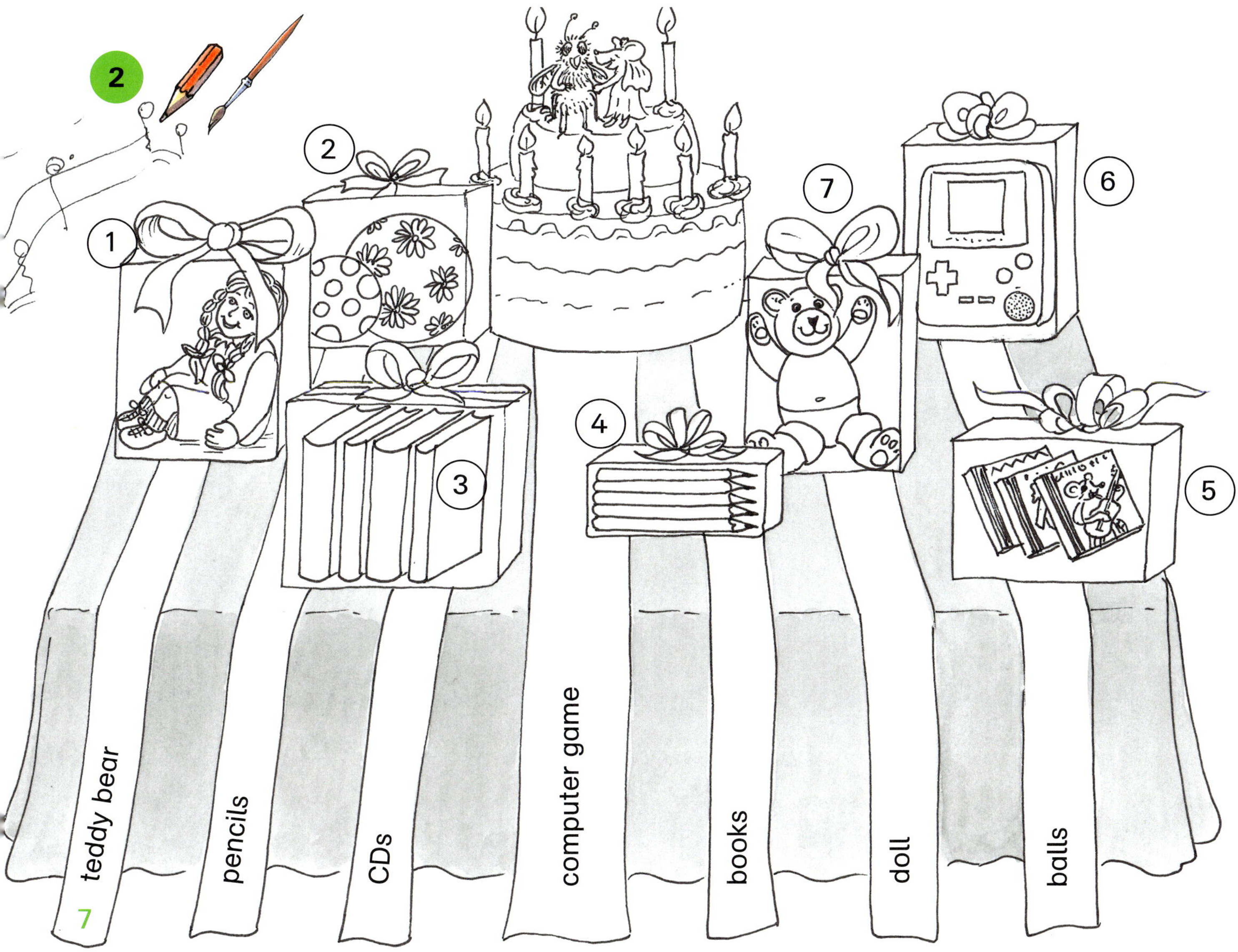

3

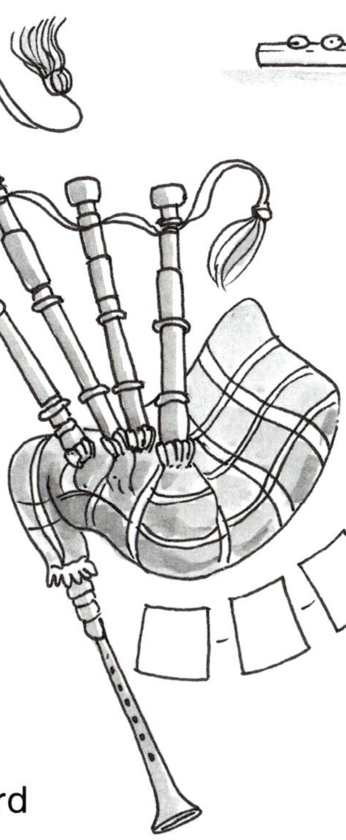

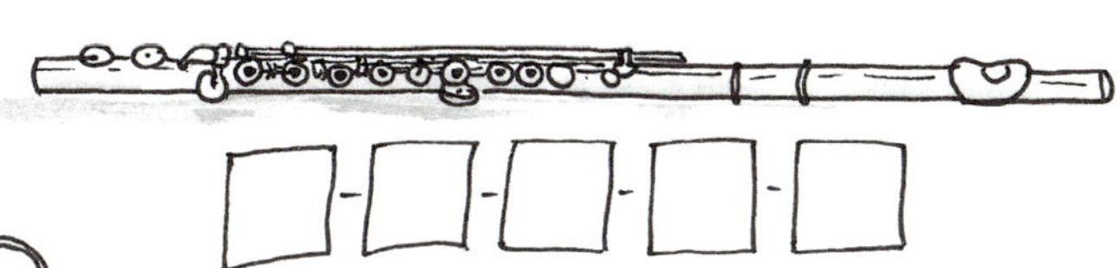

ratiug – sepipgab – etulf – murd

Down by the station

Down by the station early in the morning,
See the little puffer bellies all in a row.
See the engine driver pull the little throttle.
Chug! Chug! Puff! Puff! Off they go.

down	drunten
station	Bahnhof
early	früh
in the morning	morgens
see	sehen
little	klein
puffer bellies	Lokomotiven
in a row	in einer Reihe
engine driver	Lokomotivführer
pull	ziehen
throttle	Drosselventil

1

_______________ _______________ _______________ _______________

2

I go on holiday by ______________. I go on holiday by ______________.

I go on holiday by ______________. I go on holiday by ______________.

I go on holiday by ______________. I go on holiday by ______________.

3

In France they speak ____________________.

In Germany they speak ____________________.

In Italy they speak ____________________.

In England they speak ____________________.

Higgelty, piggelty, pop

Higglety, pigglety, pop!
The dog has eaten the mop.
The pig's in a hurry.
The cat's in a flurry.
Higglety, pigglety, pop!

Higgletum, piggletum, dee!
The farmer is milking the bee.
The horse makes the honey.
The cow thinks it's funny.
Higgletum, piggletum, dee!

Higglety, pigglety, boo!
The chickens are learning to moo.
Pigs dance on two legs.
The sheep lay the eggs.
Higglety, pigglety, boo!

dog	Hund	is milking	melkt	chickens	Hühner
has eaten	hat gefressen	bee	Biene	are learning	lernen
mop	Mop	horse	Pferd	moo	muhen
pig	Schwein	make honey	Honig geben	dance	tanzen
in a hurry	in Eile	cow	Kuh	legs	Beine
in a flurry	nervös	think	denken	sheep	Schafe
farmer	Bauer	funny	lustig	lay eggs	Eier legen

1

coffee •

• spaghetti

pizza •

• tea

cornflakes •

• chips

lemonade •

• water

chicken •

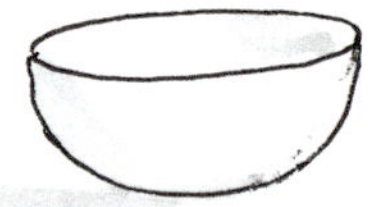

• muesli

2

grapes

~~honey~~

plums

apple

juice

milk

ice-cream

lolly

carrots

water

peppers

tomatoes

honey

____

____

____

____

____

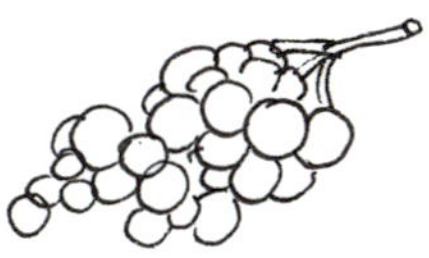

____

____

____

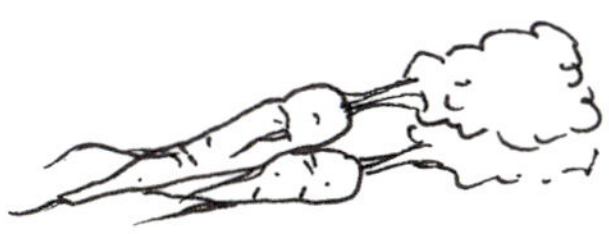

____

____

____

3

drinks	fruit	vegetables	sweets
______________	apple	______________	______________
______________	______________	______________	______________
______________	______________	______________	______________

At the circus

1 Paint the clowns.

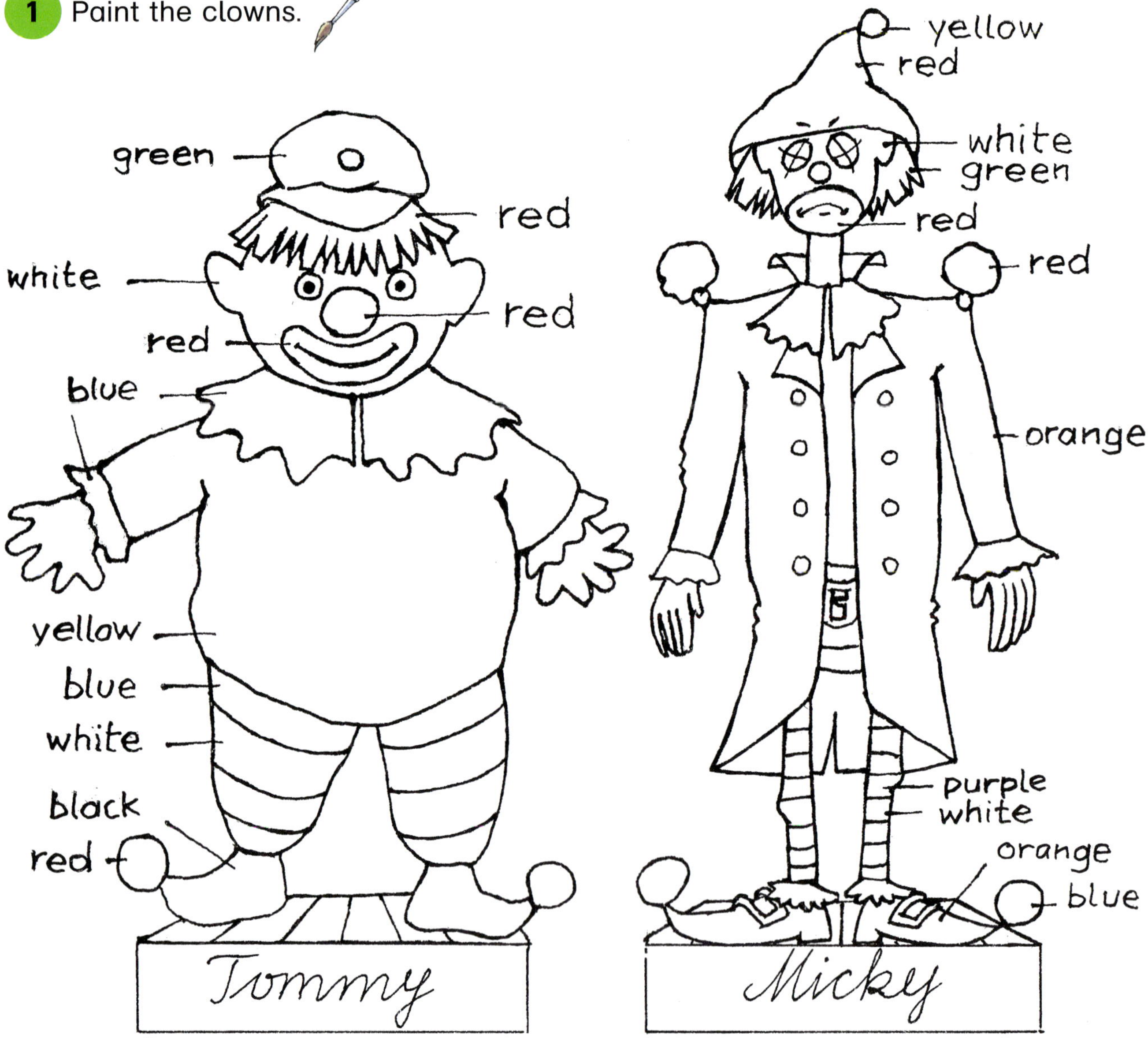

fat

2  Fill in.

~~fat~~ tall thin small sad happy

3

dry — wet

hot

clean

cold

dirty

old

young

fast

slow

4

A	B	C	D	E
			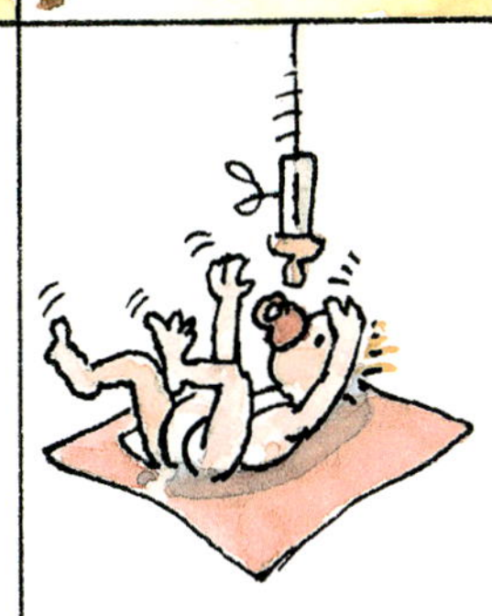	
__ __ t	__ o __ __	__ __ d	__ __ __ __ g	__ __ __ w

F	G	H	I	J

__ __ st	__ __ r __ __	__ l __ __ __	w __ __	__ __ y

In the classroom

1

a)

14	4	1	3	5	4	13

b)

2	8	1	3	7	2	10	1	13	11

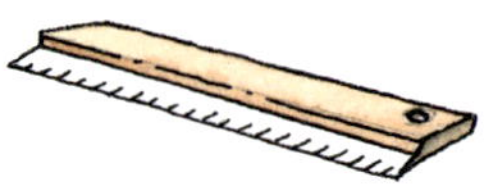

c)

13	15	8	4	13

d)

13	15	2	2	4	13

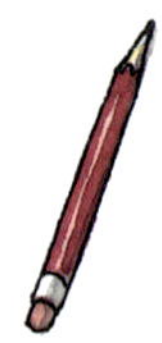

e)

12	4	9	3	6	8

f)

2	10	10	7

g)

3	5	1	6	13

h)

16	1	14	3	5	4	8

i)

14	1	2	8	4

2  Where is it?

The book is  the satchel.

in

on

under

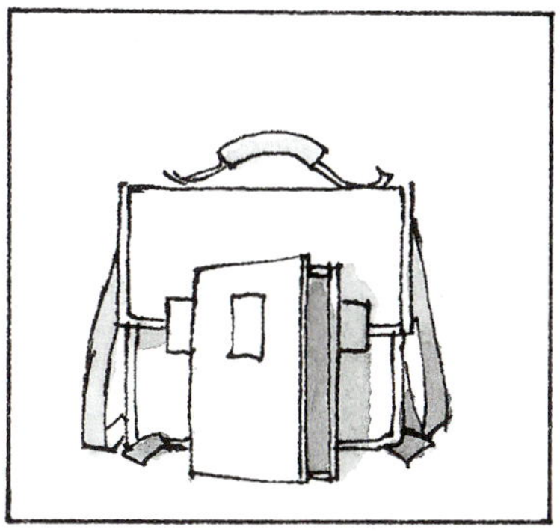
in front of

behind

beside

3  Write 5 sentences!

1) Lilly is on the table.
2) ____________________
3) ____________________
4) ____________________
5) ____________________
6) ____________________

In the living room

1

armchair lamp sofa flowers window

television (TV) newspaper telephone

2  Right or wrong?

	right	wrong
a) Susan's watching TV.		
b) David's arranging flowers.		
c) The cat's sleeping under the table.		
d) Daddy's reading the newspaper.		
e) Susan's talking on the phone.		
f) Mummy's painting a picture.		
g) Susan's sitting in the armchair.		
h) Daddy's sitting on the sofa.		
i) Mother's arranging flowers.		
j) David's talking on the phone.		

3 Which four things aren't in the living room? Cross them out.

In the garden

1 What are they doing?

2 Fill in.

a) The dog's di _ _ _ _ _ _ a hole.

b) Susan's ________________.

c) Johnny's ________________ a lollipop.

d) Peter's ________________ a kite.

c) Mary's ________________ bubbles.

f) Jane's ________________ in the pool.

g) The baby's ________________.

3 A rhyme.

Humpty Dumpty sat on a wall.
Humpty Dumpty had a great fall.
All the King's horses
And all the King's men
Couldn't put Humpty together again.

Numbers from 20 to 100

1

40 f o r t y

50 f i f t y

30 t h i r t y

60 s i x t y

70 s e v e n t y

90 n i n e t y

80 e i g h t y

100 h u n d r e d

2 Write the numbers.

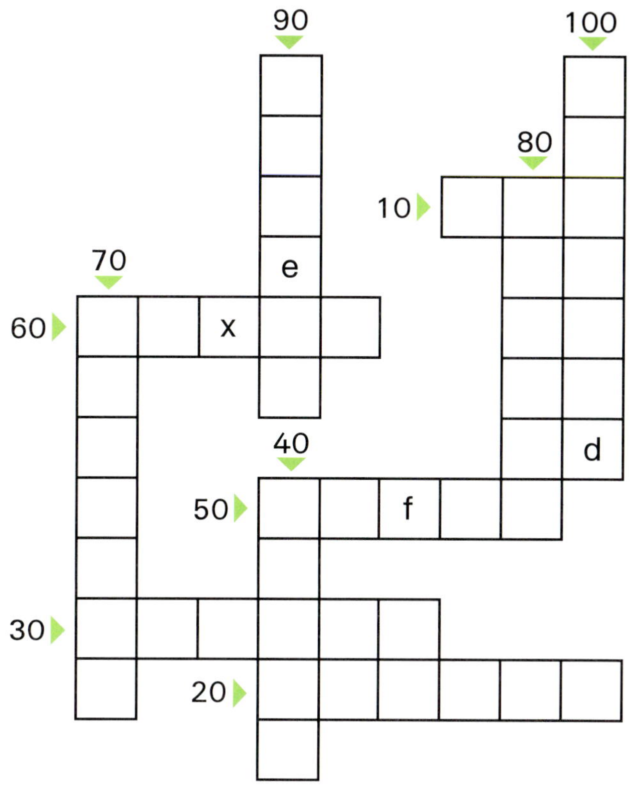

3

10 + 20 = __________

__________ plus __________ is __________

40 + 60 = __________

____

30 + 50 = __________

____

In the playground

1 What do you like doing?

I like sliding.

a) I ________

________________.

b) __ ________

________________________.

c) __ ________

________________________.

d) __ ________

________________________.

e) I like

________________________.

What do you like doing?

I ________________

________________________.

running · jumping · climbing trees · swinging · flying kites · sliding

2 Play the game.

I like sport

1

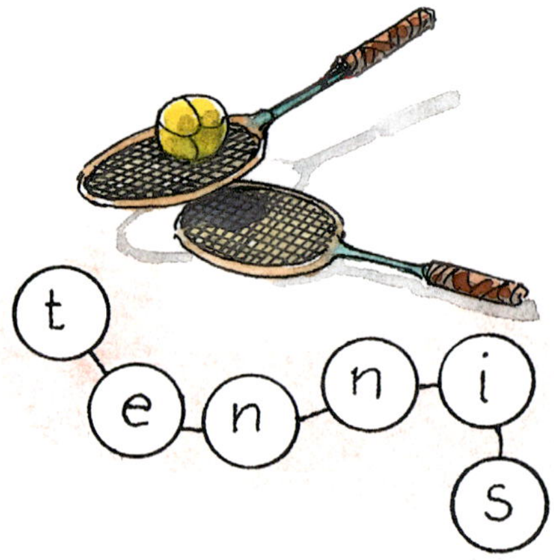

I like ______________________ and ______________________.

I like ______________________ and ______________________.

I like ______________________ and ______________________.

2 What are they doing?

They're playing

h ______________________________

They're playing

____

They're ______________________________

____

They'____ ______________________________

______________________________.

They'____ ______________________________

______________________________.

They'____ ______________________________

______________________________.

A lot to do every day

1

read

write

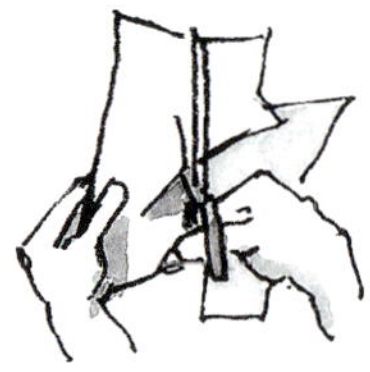
cut out

dance

cry

do maths

sing

laugh

paint

run

2 Fill in.

a) ___ ___ ___ g

b) ___ ___ a ___

c) w ___ ___ ___ ___

d) l ___ ___ ___ ___

e) ___ a ___ ___ ___

f) d ___ m ___ ___ ___ ___

g) ___ ___ i ___ ___

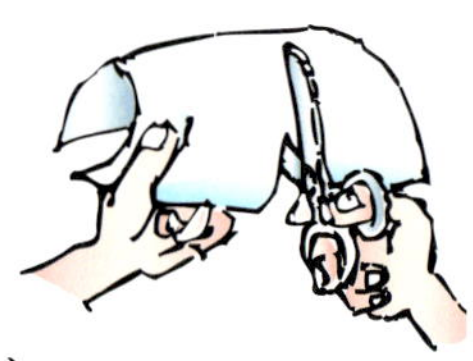
h) c ___ ___ ___ ___ t

i) c ___ ___

j) ___ ___ n

3 What do you do every day?

a) I paint every day.

b) I ________________ every day.

c) I ________________________________.

d) ________________________________.

e) ________________________________.

f) ________________________________.

So many animals

1

hen cat camel tiger dog horse lion giraffe elephant pig gorilla cow

1

2

3

4

5

6

7

8

9

10

11

12

2

a) They live on the farm:

b) They live in the zoo:

3 Count them.

two elephants

A morning at school

1 Find the right picture.

1	Susan's cutting out paper.
2	Tim's reading a book.
3	Mary's writing on the blackboard.
4	Minny's eating an apple.
5	Peter's doing maths.
6	Mary's dancing.
7	Diana's singing a song.
8	John's eating an apple.
9	Diana's painting.
10	Peter's singing a song.
11	Minny's drinking.
12	Kevin's painting.
13	Mary's painting.
14	Tim's drinking.

2 A rhyme.

Here am I,
little dancing Lizzy.
When nobody dances with me
I dance all alone.

3 Write the question.

What's Tim doing?	Tim's reading a book.
What's ______ ____________ ?	Mary's writing on the blackboard.
______________________ ?	Susan's cutting out paper.
______________________ ?	Kevin's painting a picture.
______________________ ?	Peter's doing maths.

Mrs. Smith goes shopping

1

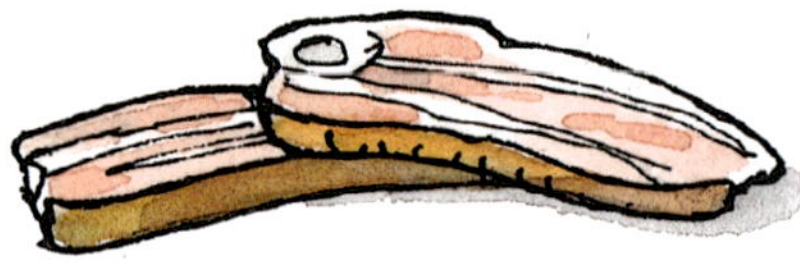

b) r ____

a) bacon

c) a loaf of b ____

bacon
chicken
loaf of bread
3 rolls
3 apples
2 bananas
2 tomatoes
6 eggs
milk

d) t ________

e) a _____

f) b ______

g) m ___

h) e ___

i) ch _____

2

Hello,
can I help
you?
I'd like a loaf of bread
and six rolls, please.

How much is it?
Three pounds
twenty, please.

Vicky's week

1

Monday

Tuesday

Wednesday

Thursday

Friday

Saturday

Sunday

a) Vicky goes to school on Monday.

b) She flies a kite on T____________________ .

c) She plays her guitar on ____________________ .

d) She feeds the ducks on ____________________ .

e) She climbs a tree on ____________________ .

f) She takes a bath on ____________________ .

g) She buys an ice-cream on ____________________ .

2

And you?

I ______________________________

______________________________ .

3 A rhyme.

How many days has my baby to play?

Sa _ _ _ _ _ _, Su _ _ _ _, Mo _ _ _ _,

Tu _ _ _ _ _, We _ _ _ _ _ _ _,

Th _ _ _ _ _ _, Fr _ _ _ _,

Sa _ _ _ _ _ _, Su _ _ _ _, Mo _ _ _ .

Hurray, hurray!
My baby wants to play
every day, every day!

Rooms in the house

1 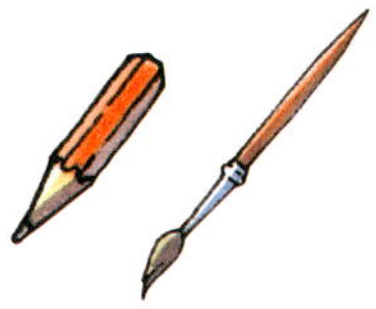

bedroom | bathroom | kitchen | living room

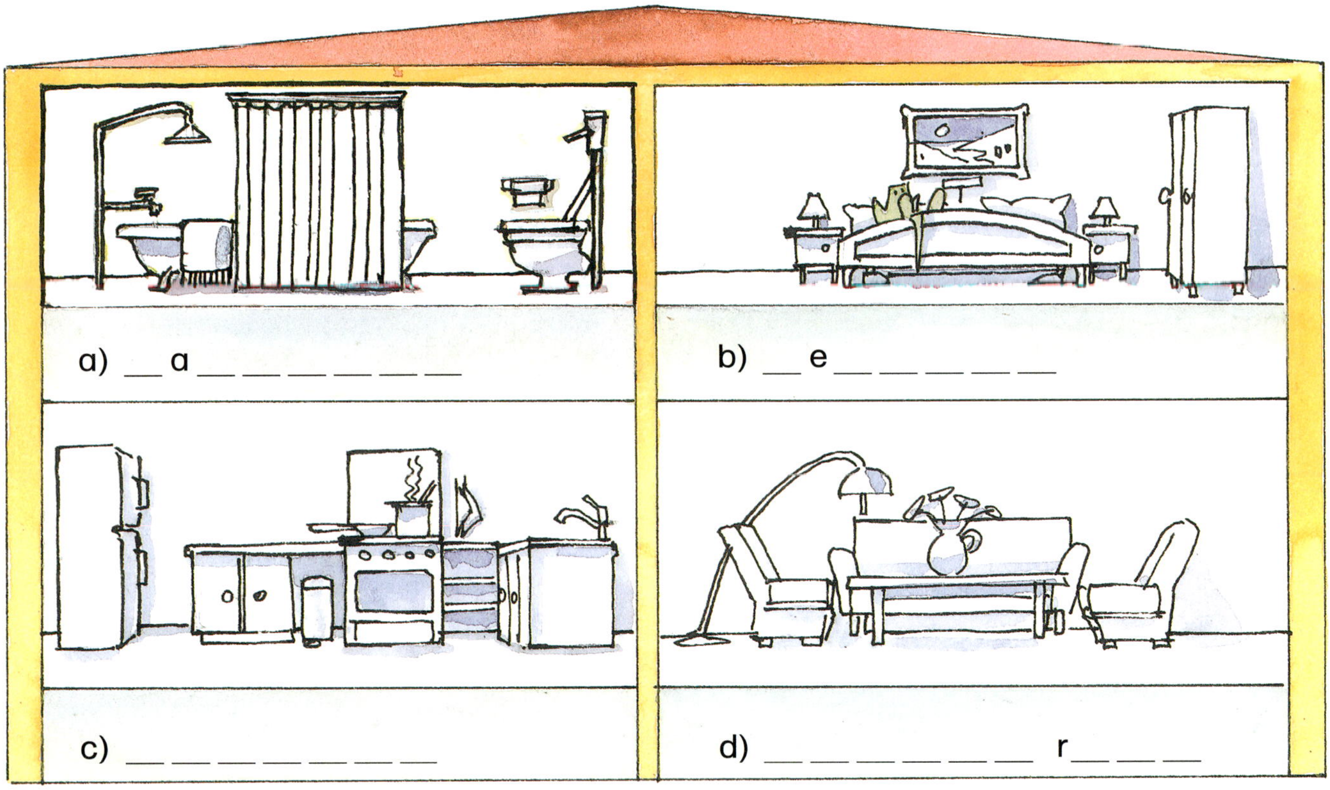

2 Where do you find them?

bed

wardrobe

bathroom

bath

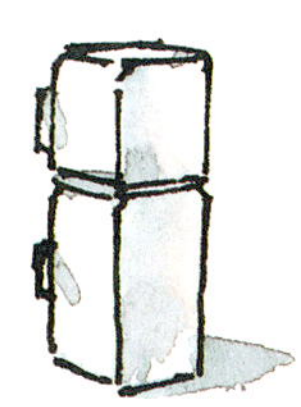
fridge

living room

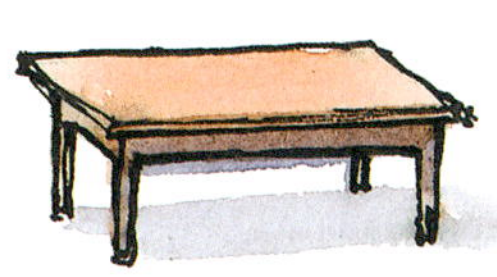
table

toilet

bedroom

kitchen

cooker

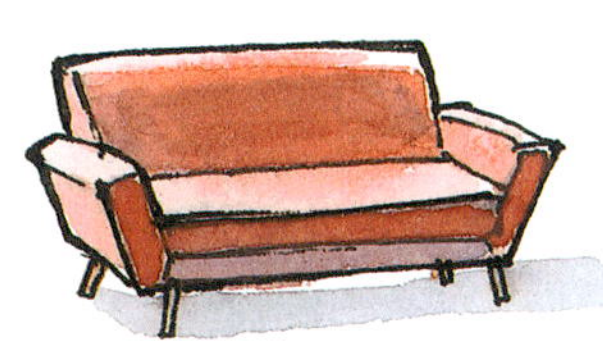
sofa

3 What do we have to do at home?

a) clean the rooms

b) wash the clothes

c) lay the table

d) wash the dishes

e) water the flowers

f) cook the meals

a) We have to clean the rooms.

b) We have to ____.

c) ____.

d) ____.

e) ____.

f) ____.

Trafic!

1 What do you see?

cars trains buses ships planes

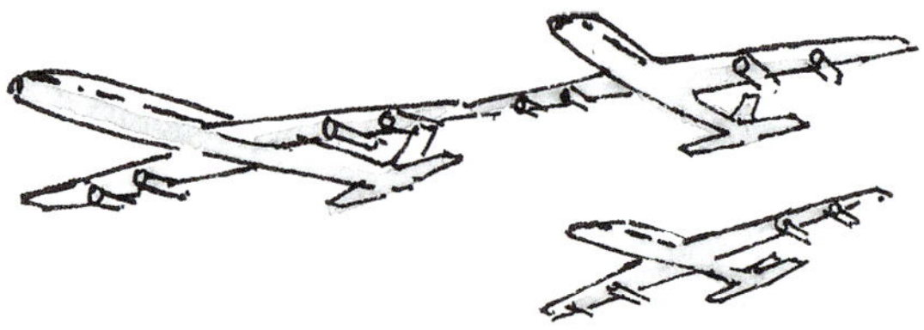

a) __ __ a __ __ __

b) __ __ r __

c) __ __ s __ __

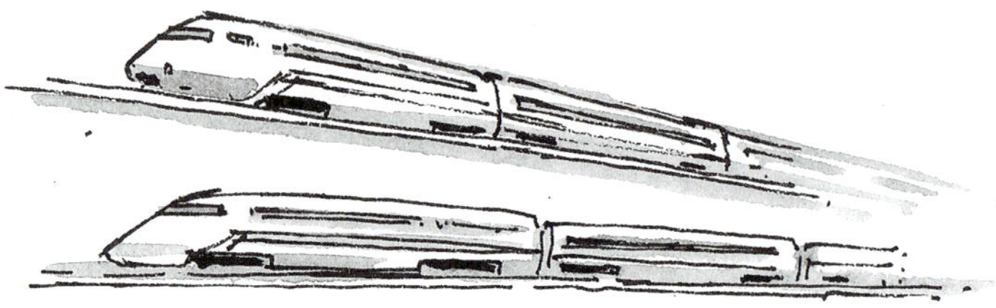

d) __ r __ __ __ __

e) __ h __ __ __

2 Where do they go?

a) Planes go to the _ _ _ _ _ _ _.

airport

b) C______ go to the _ _ _ _ _ _.

garage

c) B________ go to the _ _ _

_ _ _ _.

bus stop

d) T______ go to the _ _ _ _ _ _ _

_ _ _ _ _ _ _.

railway station

e) S______ go to the _ _ _ _.

port

A

a lot of	viele
a / an	ein, eine
(I) am / I'm	(ich) bin
again	wieder
airport	Flughafen
all	alle
and	und
animal(s)	Tier(e)
ant	Ameise
apple	Apfel
(we) are	(wir) sind
(they) are	(sie) sind
(you) are	(du) bist / (ihr) seid
arm	der Arm
armchair	Sessel
around	um herum
arrange (arranging)	ordnen
at	an, bei
at school	in der Schule
autumn	Herbst

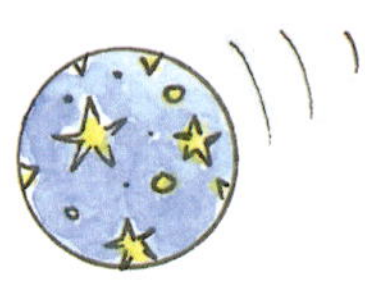

B

baby	Baby
back	zurück
bacon	Speck
ball	Ball
banana	Banane
basket	Korb
basketball	Basketball
bath	baden, das Baden
take a bath	ein Bad nehmen
bathroom	Badezimmer
bed	Bett
bedroom	Schlafzimmer
behind	hinter
beside	neben
bike	Fahrrad
bird	Vogel
birthday	Geburtstag
birthday party	Geburtstagsparty
black	schwarz
blackboard	Tafel
blouse	Bluse
blow (blowing)	blasen
blue	blau
board	Tafel
boat	Boot
body	Körper
book	Buch
bookcase	Bücherregal / Bücherschrank
box	Schachtel
boy(s)	Junge(n)
bread	Brot
a loaf of bread	ein Laib Brot
breakfast	Frühstück
brother	Bruder
brown	braun
bubble	Blase (z. B. Seifenblase)
bus	der Bus
bus stop	Bushaltestelle
buy	kaufen
Bye!	Tschüss!

C

camel	Kamel
can	können
cap	Mütze
car	Auto
carrot	Karotte
cat	Katze
CD	CD
chair	Stuhl
chest	Brust
chicken	Huhn
chips	Pommes frites
chocolate	Schokolade
Christmas	Weihnachten
classroom	Klassenzimmer
clean	sauber
climb	klettern
clock	Uhr
two o'clock	zwei Uhr
clothes	Kleidungsstücke / Kleidung
cloud	Wolke
clown	Clown
coffee	Kaffee
cold	kalt
colour(s)	Farbe(n)
computer	Computer
computer game	Computerspiel
cook	kochen
cornflakes	Cornflakes
count	zählen
cow	Kuh
crawl	kriechen / krabbeln

cross out	durchstreichen / ausstreichen
cry	weinen
cut out	schneiden

D

Dad(dy)	Papa
dance	tanzen
day	Tag
dear	liebe(r)
desk	Schreibtisch
dig (digging)	graben
dinner	Abendessen
I have dinner.	Ich esse zu Abend.
dirty	schmutzig
dishes	Geschirr
do	tun
What are they doing?	Was tun sie?
What's (= what is) he doing?	Was tut er?
do maths	rechnen
dog	Hund
doll	Puppe
dragon	Drache
draw	zeichnen
dress	Kleid
drink	trinken
drinks	Getränke
drum	Trommel
dry	trocken
duck	Ente

E

ear	Ohr
ear(s)	Ohr(en)
Easter	Ostern
eat	essen
egg	Ei
eight	acht
eighteen	achtzehn
eighty	achtzig
elephant	Elefant
eleven	elf
England	England
English	Englisch
every day	jeden Tag
everybody	jeder, alle
eye(s)	Auge(n)

F

fall	fallen; Sturz
family	Familie
farm(house)	Bauernhof
farmer	Bauer
fast	schnell
father	Vater
feed	füttern
felt tip	Filzstift
fiddle	Geige
fifteen	fünfzehn
fifty	fünfzig
fill	füllen
fill (in)	füllen
find	finden
fine	fein, gut
I am fine.	Mir geht es gut.
finger	Finger
finish	beenden
fish	Fisch
fish, fishing	fischen
five	fünf
flower	Blume
flute	Querflöte
fly (flying)	fliegen
fly a kite	einen Drachen steigen lassen
She is flying a kite.	Sie lässt einen Drachen steigen.
foot	Fuß
forty	vierzig
four	vier
fourteen	vierzehn
France	Frankreich
French	Französisch
Friday	Freitag
fridge	Kühlschrank
friend	Freund / Freundin
from	von
fruit	Früchte

G

game	Spiel
garage	Garage
garden	Garten
German	Deutsch
Germany	Deutschland
get up	aufstehen
giraffe	Giraffe
girl	das Mädchen
give	geben
glasses	Brille

glue	Kleber
go	gehen
go on	weitermachen
go shopping	einkaufen gehen
go to bed	zu Bett gehen
golf	Golf
good	gut
Good morning!	Guten Morgen!
Good night!	Gute Nacht!
Goodbye!	Auf Wiedersehen!
gorilla	Gorilla
grandfather	Großvater
grandma	Oma
grandmother	Großmutter
grandpa	Opa
grapes	Trauben
grass	Gras
great	groß
green	grün
guitar	Gitarre

H

had	hatte
hair	Haar(e)
half	halb
half past six	halb sieben
Halloween	Halloween
hamster	Hamster
hand	Hand
happy	glücklich
hat	Hut
have	haben
have lunch	Mittag essen
have to	müssen
Have you got a ...?	Hast du ein(en) ...?
have, has	haben
he	er
head	Kopf
hello	hallo
help	helfen
hen	Huhn
her	ihr(e)
here	hier / da
Here you are!	Bitte schön!
hi	hallo
his	sein(e)
hockey	Hockey
hole	Loch
holidays	Ferien
honey	Honig

hop away	wegspringen
horse	Pferd
house	Haus
how	wie
How are you?	Wie geht es dir / Ihnen?
how many	wie viele
How much is it?	Wie teuer ist das?
Humpty Dumpty	(Name)
hundred	hundert

I

I	ich
I am / I'm	ich bin
I couldn't count.	Ich konnte nicht rechnen.
I have got	ich habe
I like sliding.	Ich rutsche gerne.
I'd like ...	Ich hätte gerne ...
I'm alone.	Ich bin allein.
I'm hot.	Mir ist heiß.
ice-cream	Eis / Eiskrem
in	in
in front of	vor
is	ist
it is	es ist
he / she / it is	er / sie / es ist
Italian	Italienisch
Italy	Italien

J

jeans	Jeans
juice	Saft
jump	springen

K

king	König
kitchen	Küche
kite	(Flug-)Drachen

L

lamp	Lampe
laugh	lachen
lay the table	den Tisch decken
learn, learning	lernen
leg	das Bein
lemonade	Limonade
let's	lass uns, lasst uns
lick	lecken / schlecken

like	mögen, gern haben
lion	Löwe
little	klein
live	leben / wohnen
living room	Wohnzimmer
loaf	Laib
lollipop, lolly	Lutscher
look	sehen, schauen
Look!	Schau!
lorry	Lastwagen
lunch	Mittagessen

M

many	viele
me	mir / mich
That's me!	Das bin ich!
meal	Mahl
men	Männer
milk	Milch
Monday	Montag
monkey	Affe
more	mehr
morning	der Morgen
Good morning!	Guten Morgen!
mother	Mutter
mouse	Maus
mouth	Mund
much	viel / sehr
muesli	Müsli
mum	Mama
Mummy	Mama
must	müssen
my	mein(e)

N

name	Name
newspaper	Zeitung
nice	nett
nine	neun
nineteen	neunzehn
ninety	neunzig
no	nein
nobody	niemand
nose	Nase
not	nicht
now	nun / jetzt
number	Zahl

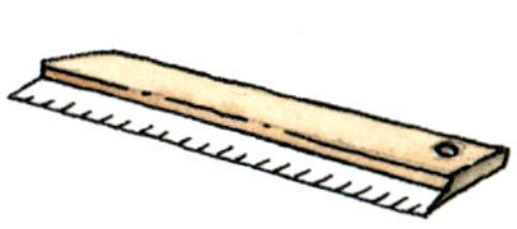

O

on	auf
on holiday	in Urlaub
one	ein(s)
old	alt
or	oder
orange	orange / (die) Orange
our	unser

P

packet	Päckchen
paint	malen
paintbox	Malkasten
paper	Papier
party	Party / Feier
pen	Füller
pencil	Bleistift
pencil case	Mäppchen
pepper	Paprika
pet	Haustier / Lieblingstier
phone	Telefon / telefonieren
phone number	Telefonnummer
picture	Bild
pig	Schwein
pink	rosa
pizza	Pizza
plane	Flugzeug
plastic bag	Plastiktüte
play	spielen
play (football)	(Fußball) spielen
playground	Spielplatz
playing tennis	Tennis spielen
please	bitte
plum	Pflaume
pony	Pony
pool (swimming pool)	Schwimmbecken
poor	arm
port	Hafen
pound	Pfund
pullover	Pullover
purple	lila
put together	zusammensetzen

Q

question	Frage

R

rabbit	Hase
radio	Radio
railway	Zug

read, reading	lesen
I am not reading	ich lese nicht
I am reading	ich lese
red	rot
reporter	Reporter
rhyme	Reim
riding a bike	Rad fahren
right	richtig / rechts
rolls	Brötchen
room	Zimmer
rubber	Radiergummi
ruler	Lineal
run	laufen

S

sad	traurig
sail, sailing	segeln
sat	saß
satchel	Schultasche
Saturday	Samstag
say	sagen
scarf	Halstuch
school	Schule
schoolbag	Schulranzen
scissors	Schere
sentence	Satz
seven	sieben
seventeen	siebzehn
seventy	siebzig
sharpener	Bleistiftspitzer
ship	Schiff
shirt	Hemd
shoe, shoes	Schuh, Schuhe
shorts	kurze Hose
sing, singing	singen
sister	Schwester
sit	sitzen
six	sechs
sixteen	sechzehn
sixty	sechzig
skateboard	Skateboard
I'm skateboarding.	Ich fahre Skateboard.
skip away	weghüpfen
sleep	schlafen
sliced	in Scheiben
slide	rutschen / Rutschbahn
slow	langsam
snake	Schlange
snow	Schnee
sock	Strumpf
socks	Socken
sofa	Sofa
song	Lied
Sorry!	Tut mir Leid!
spaghetti	Spaghetti
speak	sprechen
spider	Spinne
sport	Sport
spring	Frühling
stand	stehen
station	Bahnhof
street	Straße
summer	Sommer
sun	Sonne
Sunday	Sonntag
surf, surfing	surfen
sweets	Süßigkeiten
swim, swimming	schwimmen
swing	schaukeln

T

table	Tisch
table-tennis	Tischtennis
talk	sprechen, reden
tea	Tee
teacher	Lehrer
teddy bear	Teddybär
telephone	Telefon
television (= TV)	Fernsehen
to watch television	fernsehen
I am watching TV.	Ich sehe gerade fern.
ten	zehn
tennis	Tennis
Thank you!	Danke!
that	das dort
the	der, die, das
them	sie / ihnen
then	dann
there	dort
there are	es sind
these	diese
they	sie
thin	schlank
thing	Ding
thirteen	dreizehn
thirty	dreißig
this	dieser / diese / dieses
three	drei
Thursday	Donnerstag

tiger	Tiger
to	zu, bis
toes	Zehen
toilet	Toilette
tomato(es)	Tomate(n)
too	auch
traffic	Verkehr
train	Zug
tree	Baum
trousers	lange Hose
T-shirt	T-Shirt
Tuesday	Dienstag
TV (= television)	Fernseher
twelve	zwölf
twenty	zwanzig
two	zwei

U

under	unter

V

vegetables	Gemüse

W

wait	warten
wall	Mauer
wardrobe	Kleiderschrank
wash	waschen
watch	sehen / schauen
watching TV	fernsehen
water	Wasser
Wednesday	Mittwoch
week	Woche
weekend	Wochenende
at the weekend	am Wochenende
wet	nass
what	was / was für
what's (= what is)	was ist
when	wenn / wann
where	wo
which	welche / welches / welcher
white	weiß
who	wer
Who's (= who is) this?	Wer ist das?
wind	Wind
window	Fenster
winter	Winter
with	mit

write	schreiben
wrong	falsch

Y

year	Jahr
yellow	gelb
yes	ja
you	du
you have	du hast
your	dein(e)

Z

zoo	Zoo

Seite 4

1. Hello, John!
   Good morning, Mr. Smith!

Seite 5

1. Hello, my name is Nicky.
   Hi, my name is Donald.
   My name is Lizzy. What's your name?
   My name is Lenny.
   I am Patrick. What's your name?
   My name is ... (hier kannst du deinen eigenen Namen eintragen).

Seite 6

1. Goodbye, poor Lilian.

Seite 7

1. Yes, I'm dancing.
   I'm not skateboarding. I'm not dancing.
   I am reading.

Seite 8

1. Is Peter skateboarding? yes
   Is Julia dancing? no
   Is Dolly reading? no
2. Look, there's Dolly. She's dancing.
   Look, there's Peter. He's skateboarding.

Seite 9

1. Hello, Mary! My name is Kay.
   I am Nicky. I'm reading.
   Oh, there's Nicky. She's reading.

Seite 10/11

3. yellow, red, white, brown, green, orange
4. Chocolate is brown. An orange is orange. The sun is yellow. A tomato is red. Grass is green. Snow is white.

Seite 12/13

2. These are my friends. I've got three friends.
   These are my friends. I've got seven friends.
3. I've got ... friends. (Hier kannst du die Zahl deiner Freunde eintragen.)

Seite 14/15

1. I'm Donald. It's my birthday.
   It's his birthday.
2. I am ... years old. (Hier kannst du dein Alter eintragen.)
4. Beispiel:
   Dear Lisa!
   HAPPY BIRTHDAY to you!
   Maya

Seite 16/17

1. pink, blue, purple, black
3.

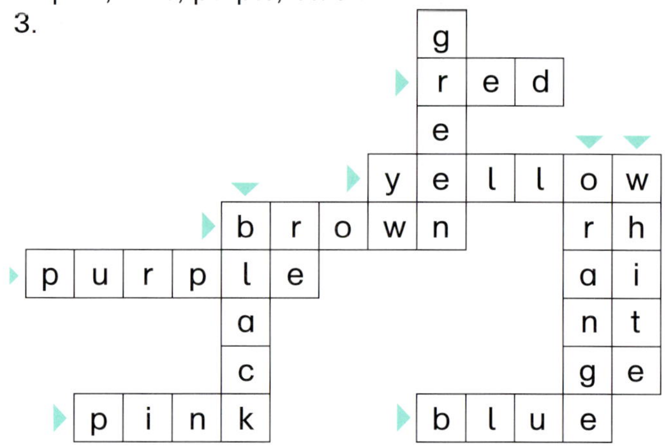

4. Toby's pullover is yellow. Toby's cap is red.
   Toby's shorts are blue. Toby's shoes are black.

Seite 18/19

1. a) dog; b) cat; c) pig; d) pony; e) hamster; f) duck; g) fish
2. I have a cat. I like my cat.
   I have a fish. I like my fish.
   I have a pig. I like my pig.
3. What pet do you have? I have ... (Hier kannst du dein Haustier eintragen.)

Seite 20/21

1. Here are three girls and there are two pencils.
   Here are three boys.
   There are four chairs.
   Here are seven books.
   There are two computers.
3. Where is the chair? The chair is beside the table.
   Where is Tommy? Tommy is on the chair.
   Where is David? David is on the table.
   Where is the little Floh? He is under the table.
   And where are you? I am ... (Hier kannst du eintragen, wo du gerade bist.)

Seite 22/23

1. hat, socks, pullover, T-shirt, dress, shoes, shorts
2. Yes. My T-shirt is red.
3. I like my red hat. I like my yellow pullover.
   I like my green shorts. I like my blue socks.

Seite 24/25

3. two eyes – one eye; two ears – one ear;
   two arms – one arm; two hands – one hand;
   two legs – one leg; two feet – one foot
4. 1) mouth; 2) finger; 3) foot; 4) arm; 5) eye; 6) leg; 7) hair; 8) hand; 9) ear; 10) nose

Seite 26/27

2. Yes, this is my sister. Her name is Nicky.
   Nicky's hair is black. Her brother's hair is brown.
3. Yes, I do. He is ten years old.
   No, I don't. I haven't any sisters or brothers.
   (oder: I haven't any brothers or sisters.)
4. My brother has a T-shirt. My grandpa has a cat.

Seite 28/29

2. This is my bed. This is my pencil. This is my kite.
   This is my ball. This is my car. This is my doll.
5. This is my ball. It is blue.
   Give me your blue ball, please.
   Here you are.

Seite 30/31

1. They go to school at eight o'clock. They play at four o'clock. They have dinner at six o'clock. They watch TV at half past six. They go to bed at half past eight. Good night!
2. I am …
   I get up at ? o'clock.
   I go to school at ? o'clock.
   I play at ? o'clock.
   I have dinner at ? o'clock.
   I watch TV at ? o'clock.
   I go to bed at ? o'clock.
   (Bei den Fragezeichen setzt du jeweils die Uhrzeit ein, zu der du die verschiedenen Dinge tust.

Seite 33

1. Six elephants went out to play,
   Out on a spider's web one day.
   They had such enormous fun,
   They called for another elephant to come.
2. elephant, dog
   spider, cat
3. yes, no, no, yes, yes

Seite 34

1.

A	Z	R	A	I	N
W	O	P	F	S	K
I	S	U	N	H	A
N	R	S	N	O	W
D	E	X	I	S	Q
I	C	L	O	U	D

Seite 35

2. spring, autumn
   summer, winter
3. Christmas is in winter.
   Easter is in spring.
   Halloween is in autumn.
   Summer holidays are in summer.

Seite 36

1.

Seite 37

2. Sara says,
   "Tom is my grandpa.
   Ann is my grandma.
   Mike is my dad.
   Susan is my mum.
   Robin is my brother.
   Kevin is my brother.
   I'm Robin and Kevin's sister."
3. → grandpa, brother, dad, mum ↓ grandma
4. She is Robin and Kevin's sister.

Seite 38

1. farm – cow – grass – ~~banana~~ – farmhouse – farmer
   dog – sheep – duck – pig – ~~train~~ – horse
   quack – woof – miaow – moo – oink – ~~hello~~

Seite 39

2.

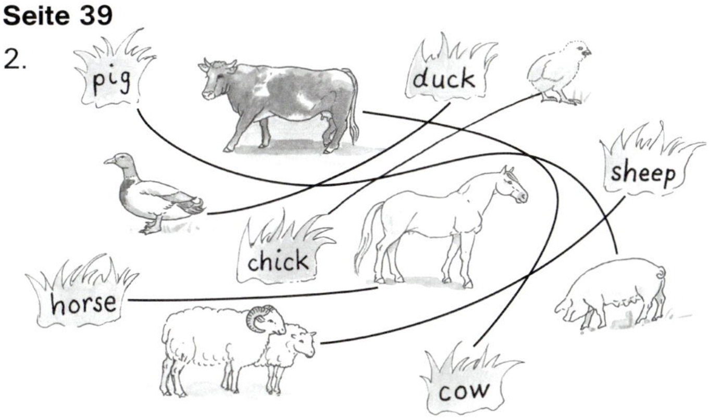

3. no, no, no, no, yes
4. two cows
   four hamsters
   three spiders
   five cats
   seven rabbits

Seite 41

1. Breakfast is at seven o'clock.
   Lunch is at one o'clock.
   Tea is at five o'clock.
   Dinner is at eight o'clock.
2. Lenny plays basketball at three o'clock.
   Lizzy has lunch at two o'clock.
   Baby Floh goes to bed at eight o'clock.

Seite 42

1. yellow/1, orange/2, white/3, pink/4, green/5, red/6, brown/7, blue/8

Seite 43

3. Her name is Ann.

Seite 44

1. The fox is in the box.
   The mouse is in the house.
   The goat is in the boat.
   The cat is in the hat.

Seite 45

3. 6 Ron
   2 Susan
   4 Mike
   3 Mandy
   5 Carol
   1 Tom

Seite 47

1. a board, a pencil case, a ruler, a schoolbag, a book
2.

				S		B					
		S	C	H	O	O	L				
				A		O					
C	H	A	I	R		K					
				P							
			P	E	N	C	I	L			
				N							
				E							
				R	U	B	B	E	R		
						O			U		D
						A		G	L	U	E
						R			E		S
						D			R		K

3. 3 rulers
   2 pencils
   4 books
   5 scissors
   1 schoolbag
   1 sharpener
   1 pencil case
   1 glue

Seite 48

Seite 49

2. h orse
   a nt
   m ouse
   s nake
   t eddy bear
   e lephant
   r abbit = hamster
3. 2 monkeys
   3 dogs
   2 ducks
   1 snake

Seite 50

1. glasses, scarf, shirt, socks, jeans, shoes

Seite 51

2.

3. One spider has got 8 legs.
   Two cows have got 8 legs.
   Three birds have got 6 legs.
   Four horses have got 16 legs.
   Five rabbits have got 20 legs.
   One duck has got 2 legs.

Seite 52

1. bumblebee  mouse

Seite 53

2. teddy bear/7, pencils/4, CDs/5, computer game/6, books/3, doll/1, balls/2
3. drum, guitar, bagpipes, flute

Seite 54

1. Italy, France, Germany, England

Seite 55

2. I go on holiday by bike/boat/bus/car/plane/train.
3. In France they speak French.
   In Germany they speak German.
   In Italy they speak Italian.
   In England they speak English.

Seite 56

1.

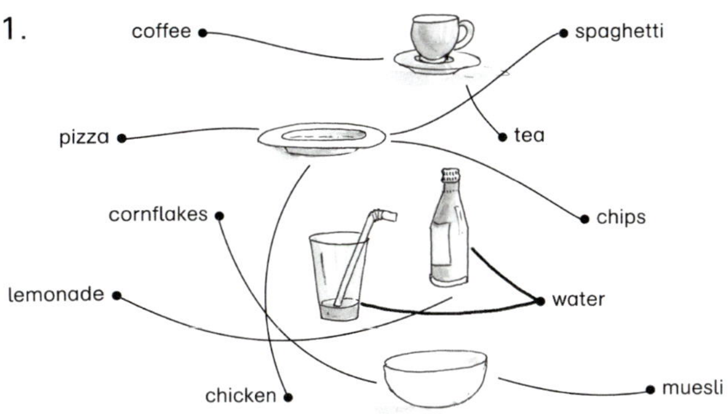

Seite 57

2. honey tomatoes juice lolly
   peppers water grapes milk
   plums carrots ice-cream apple

3. drinks: water, juice, milk
   fruit: plums, apple, grapes
   vegetables: tomatoes, peppers, carrots
   sweets: honey, ice-cream, lolly

Seite 58/59

2. Tommy: fat, small, happy; Micky: tall, thin, sad
4. A: hot; B: cold; C: old; D: young; E: slow; F: fast; G: dirty; H: clean; I: wet; J: dry

Seite 60/61

1. a) teacher; b) blackboard; c) ruler; d) rubber; e) pencil; f) book; g) chair; h) satchel; i) table
3. Beispiele: Lilly (or: a girl) is on the table. Mr. Smith (or: the teacher) is in front of the blackboard. Julian (or: a boy) is in front of the table. The rubber is on the table. The satchel is under the table. The ruler is in the satchel. The book is in the satchel.

Seite 62/63

2. right: c), d), e), h), i); wrong: a), b), f), g), j)
3. These things are not in the living room: pencil, dog, radio, satchel

Seite 64/65

2. a) The dog's digging a hole.
   b) Susan's laughing.
   c) Johnny's licking a lollipop.
   d) Peter's flying a kite.
   e) Mary's blowing bubbles.
   f) Jane's swimming in the pool.
   g) The baby's crawling.

Seite 66/67

1. 30: thirty; 40: forty; 50: fifty; 60: sixty; 70: seventy; 80: eighty; 90: ninety; 100: hundred
2.

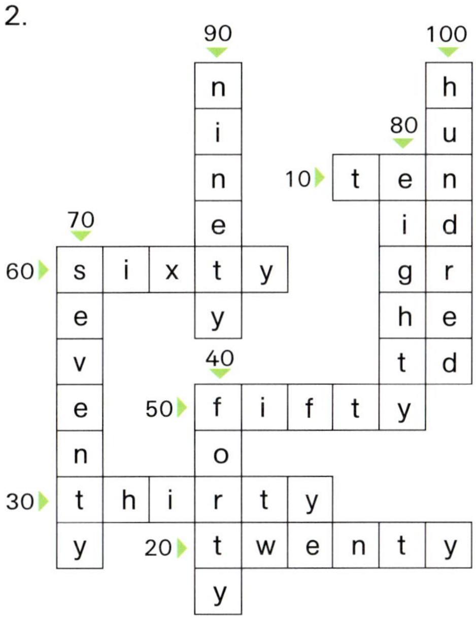

3.

10 +	20	=	30	
ten plus	twenty is		thirty	
40 +	60	=	100	
forty	plus	sixty	is	a hundred
30 +	50	=	80	
thirty	plus	fifty	is	eighty

Seite 68/69

1. a) I like running. b) I like jumping.
   c) I like climbing trees. d) I like swinging.
   e) I like flying kites.
   What do you like doing? Beispiel: I like sliding.

Seite 70/71

1. I like hockey and tennis.
   I like golf and basketball.
   I like table-tennis and football.
2. 1) They're playing hockey.
   2) They're playing golf.

3) They're playing basketball.
4) They're playing table-tennis.
5) They're playing tennis.
6) They're playing football.

Seite 72/73

2. a) sing; b) read; c) write; d) laugh; e) dance; f) do maths; g) paint; h) cut out; i) cry; j) run
3. a) I paint every day. b) I write every day. c) I cut out every day. d) I sing every day. e) I laugh every day. f) I read every day.

Seite 74/75

1.

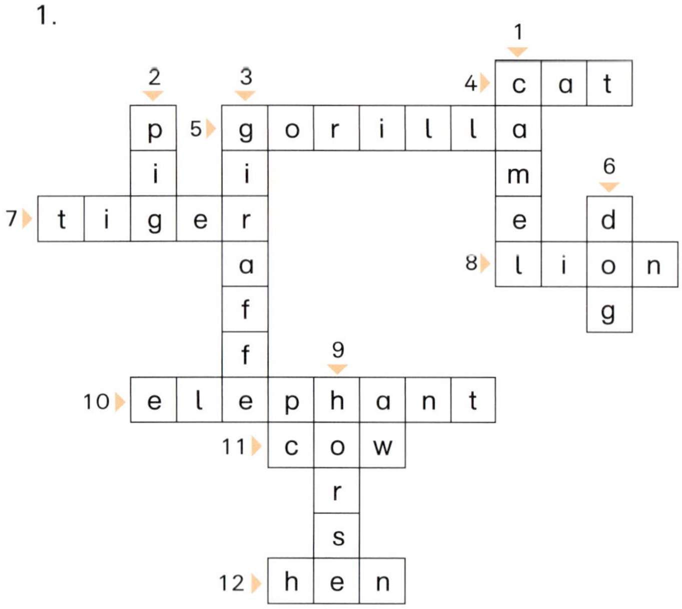

2. a) They live on the farm: cat, dog, pig, hen, horse, cow
   b) They live in the zoo: camel, gorilla, lion, tiger, elephant, giraffe
3. two elephants, four gorillas, three giraffes, six lions

Seite 76/77

1. 1 Tim's reading a book. 2 Mary's writing on the blackboard. 5 Susan's cutting out paper. 7 Minny's drinking. 8 John's eating an apple. 9 Peter's doing maths. 11 Kevin's painting. 13 Diana's singing a song.
3. What's Mary doing? What's Susan doing? What's Kevin doing? What's Peter doing?

Seite 78/79

1. a) bacon; b) rolls; c) a loaf of bread; d) tomatoes; e) apples; f) bananas; g) milk; h) eggs; i) chicken

Seite 80/81

1. a) Vicky goes to school on Monday.
   b) She flies a kite on Tuesday.
   c) She plays her guitar on Wednesday.
   d) She feeds the ducks on Thursday.
   e) She climbs a tree on Friday.
   f) She takes a bath on Saturday.
   g) She buys an ice-cream on Sunday.
2. (Hier kannst du aufschreiben, was du an Wochenenden üblicherweise tust.) Beispiele: At weekends I read a book. At weekends I play with my friends.
3. How many days has my baby to play?
   Saturday, Sunday, Monday,
   Tuesday, Wednesday,
   Thursday, Friday,
   Saturday, Sunday, Monday.
   Hurray, hurray!
   My baby wants to play
   every day, every day!

Seite 82/83

1. a) bathroom; b) bedroom; c) kitchen; d) living room
2. bathroom: bath, toilet; living room: table, sofa; bedroom: wardrobe, bed; kitchen: fridge, cooker
3. a) We have to clean the rooms. b) We have to wash the clothes. c) We have to lay the table. d) We have to wash the dishes. e) We have to water the flowers. f) We have to cook the meals.

Seite 84/85

1. a) planes; b) cars; c) buses; d) trains; e) ships
2. a) Planes go to the airport.
   b) Cars go to the garage.
   c) Buses go to the bus stop.
   d) Trains go to the railway station.
   e) Ships go to the port.